EASTMAN SCHOOL OF MUSIC SERIES

Basic Principles of the Technique of 18th and 19th Century Composition

EASTMAN SCHOOL OF MUSIC SERIES

BASIC PRINCIPLES OF THE TECHNIQUE OF 18TH AND 19TH CENTURY COM-
POSITION By Allen Irvine McHose

SIGHT-SINGING MANUAL By Allen Irvine McHose & Ruth Northup Tibbs

THE CONTRAPUNTAL HARMONIC TECHNIQUE OF THE 18TH CENTURY
By Allen Irvine McHose

KEYBOARD AND DICTATION MANUAL
By Allen Irvine McHose & Donald F. White

CHORALE COLLECTION By Elvera Wonderlich

TEACHERS DICTATION MANUAL By Allen Irvine McHose

DIRECT APPROACH TO COUNTERPOINT IN SIXTEENTH CENTURY STYLE
By Gustave Fredric Soderlund

EXAMPLES OF GREGORIAN CHANT AND WORKS BY ORLANDUS LASSUS,
GIOVANNI PIERLUIGI PALESTRINA, AND MARC ANTONIO INGEGNERI
By Gustave Fredric Soderlund

EXAMPLES ILLUSTRATING THE DEVELOPMENT OF MELODIC LINE AND
CONTRAPUNTAL STYLE FROM GREEK MELODY TO MOZART
By Gustave Fredric Soderlund

THE ART OF ORCHESTRATION By Bernard Rogers

HANDBOOK OF CONDUCTING By Karl Van Hoesen

EXAMPLES OF MUSIC BEFORE 1400 By Harold Gleason

METHOD OF ORGAN PLAYING By Harold Gleason

A MODERN METHOD FOR THE DOUBLE BASS By Nelson Watson

BASIC
PRINCIPLES OF
THE TECHNIQUE OF
18th and 19th century
COMPOSITION

By

ALLEN IRVINE McHOSE

New York

APPLETON-CENTURY-CROFTS, INC.

To

Howard Hanson

Preface

For many years there has been considerable thought given to the welding together, for a first-year course in the theory of music, of the individual courses in keyboard harmony, sight-singing, dictation, and the so-called "paper work." It is the belief of many thoughtful musicians that if these courses with their special achievements could be integrated, the progress of the student would be more rapid, the student's musicianship would be more sound, and his evaluation of his own training would have more meaning. Experience has taught us that, in order to make this correlation, some common denominator is necessary. This common denominator, for 18th and 19th century music, is the theory of chord progression.

The theoretical basis for this text is found in an almost unbroken chain of musicians. Some were a combination of composer, theoretician, and scholar of physics; others were physicists interested in applying acoustical data to a better understanding of the art of music. In the first group are such men as Gioseffe Zarlino, Jean Philippe Rameau, and Friedrich Marpurg; in the second are François Joseph Fétis, Moritz Hauptmann, and Hermann Helmholtz. It is unfortunate that so little attention has been paid by the authors in the field of theory to these pioneers who have established the basis for our aural comprehension of 18th and 19th century compositions.

As the course unfolds itself, the student will become increasingly conscious of the fact that the theoretical basis for this period remains constant. The theory that enables him to identify an element is also the very same theory that enables him to use this element in a creative way.

The *Basic Principles of the Technique of 18th and 19th Century Composition* is designed to develop the musical thought processes by correlating keyboard harmony, dictation, sight-singing, and part-writing. Each element of the period is presented according to the following plan:

1. Theoretical discussion
2. Experience by creating the element (keyboard and sight-singing)
3. Dictation (aural perception)
4. Artistic application (composition)

vii

Following the Introduction, the text is divided into two parts.   Part I presents the elements of time and rhythm.   Part II begins with a study of the tonal elements of the period, in Chapters 13 to 18.   Chapters 19 to 33 combine the elements of time and rhythm with tonal elements to further a study of tonality.

A proposed schedule for the presentation of the material for five class periods a week is as follows:

First Semester

Introduction   Part I   Part II
                 Chapters 1 through 7   Chapters 13 through 25

Second Semester

     Part I   Part II
Chapters 8 through 12   Chapters 26 through 33

In addition to this text, the student must have the *Sight-Singing Manual*, McHose and Tibbs, Appleton-Century-Crofts, Inc., which contains all the correlated material which is assigned in the exercises.   The present text is likewise correlated with the *Teachers Dictation Manual*, McHose, Appleton-Century-Crofts, Inc.   The author suggests that additional sight-singing material be made available for classroom drills in rhythmic reading and sight-singing, using the following collections:

> *Folk Song Sight-Singing Series*, Books I through IX (Oxford University Press, London; Carl Fischer, Inc., New York).
> *Clarendon Song Books*, Vol. I through Vol. VI (Oxford University Press, London; Carl Fischer, Inc., New York).

This text is designed for a class of not less than ten and not more than fifteen. It has been the author's experience that keeping a class to this number insures individual participation, promotes class discussion, and makes possible the right kind of competition.   If the book is to be used for private instruction, it is advisable to use at least two periods a week.

A real debt of gratitude is owed to Dr. Howard Hanson, first, because he is one of the original champions of correlated theoretical presentation, and secondly, for the enthusiastic support and guidance which he has given the author and his colleagues in making this text possible; to Ruth Northup Tibbs, Elvera Wonderlich, Donald White, and Thomas Canning for their aid and constructive criticism in the preparation of the book; to Appleton-Century-Crofts for their permission to use the conductor's beat diagrams from the *Handbook of Conducting*, by Karl Van Hoesen; to the staff of the Sibley Library of the Eastman School of Music; to the graduate assistants who aided in collecting the many musical examples; and finally, to my secretary, Miss Mildred Burton, who helped prepare the final typescript.

A. I. McH.

Contents

ix

Introduction

ELEMENTARY ACOUSTICS*

The *Art of Music* has one of its roots in the physicist's laboratory. Gioseffe Zarlino (1517–1590), noted composer and theoretician, concluded that the art of music is neither purely mathematical nor purely a natural expression of the tone-poet. Music is the result of a happy compromise of both.

The study of sound, its source, its transmission, and its effect on the auditory nerve is called *acoustics*. It is, therefore, proper that this study begin by considering the effect of *energy* on *matter*. *Matter* occupies space. It is everything that we can touch, see, and taste. *Energy* is the agency for producing any change in the motion or condition of matter. Matter is said to possess energy when, by reason of its position or condition, it is capable of doing work. Water in an elevated reservoir, the stringed instrument's bow, the percussion player's drum sticks, the air in a bellows, and the air in the lungs of a brass instrumentalist are all examples of matter ready to do work. Energy can neither be created nor destroyed. It can be transmitted from one body to another. This concept is the basis of the production of sound.

THE SOURCE OF SOUND

Bodies are said to be *elastic* if they return to their original form after being acted upon by some external force. Music uses elastic matter. Sound originates in a vibrating elastic body. The most elementary example of a vibrating body may be illustrated by the pendulum.

The ball *B* is suspended from the point *A* and represents the pendulum *AB* at rest. If the pendulum is set in motion, it will return at regular time intervals to the starting-point *AB*. A complete or double vibration is the motion of the pendu-

* If possible, precede the study of the Introduction by showing the sound film, "Sound Waves and Their Sources," released by Encyclopaedia Britannica Films, University of Chicago, Chicago, Ill.

3

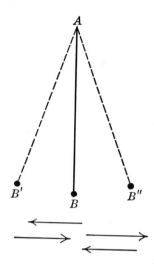

lum between two successive passages of the moving body through any point of its path in the same direction. For example, starting at B the path moves to B', returns to B, continues to B'', and finally returns to B. This complete journey of the ball is known as a *double vibration*. When a body vibrates according to the principle of the pendulum, it vibrates *transversely*. Strings of a violin, wires of a piano, and reeds of an old-fashioned cabinet organ vibrate transversely. It is to be noted in the above illustration that a body vibrates transversely when its motion is at right angles to its length.

Not all elastic bodies, however, vibrate transversely. A column of air vibrates in quite a different manner. The following straight line of dots represents particles of air at rest in a column of air in a tube.

$A \cdot$ $\cdot$ $\cdot$ $\cdot$ $\cdot$ $\cdot$ $\cdot$ $\cdot$ $\cdot$ $\cdot$ $\cdot$ $\cdot$ $\cdot B$

Disturb the column of air in the tube by blowing air across one end of the tube or by rubbing the tube with a damp cloth. Vibrations will be set up in the tube and the particles of air will move back and forth along the same line in the following manner:

$A \cdot \cdot \overset{x}{\cdot\cdot\cdot} \cdot \cdot \underset{y}{\cdot} \cdot \cdot \cdot \overset{x}{\cdot\cdot\cdot} \cdot \cdot \underset{y}{\cdot} \cdot \cdot \cdot \overset{x}{\cdot\cdot} \cdot \cdot B$

As this forward and backward motion of the particles of air takes place, periods of compression and rarefaction take place. The areas of compression are at x; the areas of rarefaction are at y. A body vibrates *longitudinally* when the particles of a body move forward and backward in the direction of its length. The air columns found in organ pipes, brass instruments, and woodwind instruments vibrate longitudinally.

THE TRANSMISSION OF SOUND

WAVE MOTION

Simple wave motion is best illustrated by attaching a flexible rope, about eight feet long, to a fixed support. By stretching the rope horizontally and starting a disturbance by an up-and-down motion of the hand, the observer will notice that a series of like geometrical figures, resembling water waves in that they have a crest and trough, will travel along the rope from the hand to the fixed end. The particles that make up the rope do not travel from one end to the other; these particles move only up and down, in the same manner as the arm which set up the disturbance. This means that each particle of the rope has its own periodic vibration. This progressive change of form, due to the periodic vibration of the particles of the rope, forms the *wave*. No two particles of the rope are in the same stage of vibration. What they actually do is to pass through corresponding positions in succession. The position of a particle of a vibrating body at any moment as a wave is being generated is called its *phase*.

When the vibrating particles move at right angles to the direction in which the wave is traveling, the wave is called *transverse*.

When the vibrating particles move to and fro in the same direction as the wave is traveling, the wave is called *longitudinal*.

Transverse wave

Longitudinal wave

In actual practice, the physicist uses the picture of the transverse wave to depict also the longitudinal wave, a convention which will be observed in this chapter. Those portions of the curve above the axis represent displacements to the right (compressions); those below the axis represent displacements to the left (rarefactions).

The *wavelength* is the distance between two particles having the same phase. For example, in the longitudinal wave the length is measured from a point of maximum compression to the next point of maximum compression, or from a point of maximum rarefaction to the next point of maximum rarefaction. In the transverse wave the length is measured along a line parallel to the axis, or rest line, from the maximum point of one crest to the maximum point of the next crest; from the minimum point of one trough to the minimum point of the next trough; or from the point at which the wave crosses the rest line to the point where the wave, going in the same direction, again crosses the rest line.

Sound is that kind of disturbance in an elastic medium which is capable of exciting the auditory sensory organ. A body, when it is acted upon by an external force, vibrates either transversely or longitudinally. This vibrating body, when surrounded by an elastic medium such as air, transmits its energy through the medium in longitudinal waves. These waves are called *sound waves*. It is the action of these waves as they are picked up by the ear which produces the sensation of hearing.

During the 19th century physicists investigating the transmission of sound discovered that the *velocity of sound waves* in air at 68° Fahrenheit is approximately 1131 feet per second.

REFLECTION

If sound waves come in contact with matter whose density is greater than that of the medium through which they are traveling, the sound waves may be *reflected*. This may be illustrated by throwing a tennis ball against a hard surface. If the ball is thrown perpendicular to the surface, it will return in the same path that it was thrown. If it is thrown at an angle, it will be reflected at an angle which is equal to the angle of incidence.

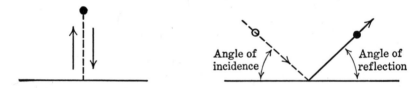

Practically all types of reflecting surfaces absorb some of the sound waves. For this reason, reflected sound is weaker. An echo is a familiar illustration of *reflected sound waves*. A cliff, a wooded hill, or the side of a large building are excellent reflecting surfaces.

RESONANCE

The accompanying illustration shows three pendulums, p^1, p^2, and p^3. p^1 and p^3 have the same length, and p^2 is shorter.

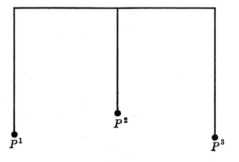

If p^1 is set in motion, after a short time p^3 will begin to swing to and fro. Increasing the energy of p^1 will not affect the dormant condition of p^2, but p^3 will continue its motion. If two bodies have the same period of vibration, one of the bodies is capable of absorbing the energy of the other which is in motion. This phenomenon is called *sympathetic vibration*. If the connection between p^1 and p^2 is firm enough, p^2 may be forced to follow the vibration of p^1. This occurrence is called *forced vibration*. The sounding boards of stringed instruments are firmly coupled to the vibrating strings and thus vibrate with frequencies determined by the strings. The f-holes in the sounding board of a violin permit the air inside the body of the violin to vibrate sympathetically. By this process, sounds produced on a stringed instrument can be heard at greater distances. This is caused by the fact that the air surrounding the body of the violin is set in motion, as well as the air surrounding the vibrating string. The physical term applied to this phenomenon is *resonance*. The reënforcement of sound by the union of direct and reflected waves is resonance.

MUSICAL SOUND

Sounds which are used in music are classified as either *musical sounds* or *noise*. The characteristics of a musical sound are *pitch*, *intensity*, and *quality*. Noise, from the standpoint of the musician, lacks definite pitch, but may possess intensity and, to some degree of discernment, quality.

PITCH

The *pitch* of any vibrating generator is determined by the number of complete vibrations which reach the ear per second. This number of complete vibrations per second is called *frequency*. Low pitches have frequencies of smaller numbers, and higher pitches have frequencies of larger numbers. The lowest tone on the piano has a frequency of 27.5 vibrations per second; the highest tone on the piano has a frequency of 4186 vibrations per second. Every pitch has its own wavelength. A thirty-two-foot open pipe in a pipe organ, whose frequency is 17.7 vibrations per second, has a wavelength of sixty-four feet; an open pipe ¾ of an inch in length, whose frequency is 9050 vibrations per second, has a wavelength of 1.5 inches.*

Musicians derive sound from two main sources: *vibrating strings* and *vibrating air columns*. A secondary source of frequencies suitable for musicians is derived from *vibrating rods, reeds, plates*, and *membranes*.

---

* When the velocity of sound waves in air is known and the length of an open or closed organ pipe is known, the frequency produced by either pipe can be calculated by the following formulas:

$$\text{frequency} = \frac{\text{velocity of sound (ft. per second)}}{2 \times \text{length of open pipe (ft.)}}$$

$$= \frac{\text{velocity of sound (ft. per second)}}{4 \times \text{length of closed pipe (ft.)}}$$

The frequencies cited in the text are based on the velocity of sound at 68° F. (1131 ft. per second).

The determining factors which control the pitch of strings are length, tension, diameter, and density.   In 1636, Mersenne's *Harmonie Universelle* listed the following laws of vibrating strings:

1. Tension, diameter, and density remain constant.
   The pitch is inversely proportional to the length of the string.   (The shorter the string, the higher the pitch.)
2. Length, diameter, and density remain constant.
   The pitch is proportional to the square root of the tension to which the string is subjected.   (The greater the tension, the higher the pitch.)
3. Length, tension, and density remain constant.
   The pitch varies inversely as the diameter of the string.   (The greater the diameter, the lower the pitch.)
4. Length, tension, and diameter remain constant.
   The pitch is inversely proportional to the square root of the density of the string. (Substitute a wire string for a gut string, keeping the same length, tension, and diameter.   The resulting pitch will be lower.)

A careful study of the string instruments will help to make these laws clear to the student.

The determining factor which controls the pitch of an air column is length. The basic law is as follows: The pitch is inversely proportional to the length of the air column.   The shorter the organ pipe, the higher the pitch.   The above law, although correct, must be modified clearly to take care of the fact that, in the case of musical instruments, the tubes which contain the air column may be open at both ends or closed at one end.   Musicians use open and closed pipes.   For example, an open eight-foot organ pipe has a frequency of 70.7 vibrations per second.   If that same pipe is stopped at one end, it will produce a frequency of 35.3 vibrations per second.   Now, an open pipe of 16 feet will also produce a frequency of 35.3 vibrations per second.   Under these circumstances, an organ builder, when working in a limited space, could easily use this acoustical law to obtain low frequencies when the ceiling of the organ chamber will not permit the use of open sixteen-foot pipes.   It must be understood, however, that stopping a pipe also has an affect on the quality of sound, and this fact will be discussed later in this introduction.

The *wavelength* of the sound produced by an open organ pipe is *twice the length of the pipe*.   This law is based on the theory of stationary waves.   Two waves of equal length and equal amplitude, traveling in opposite directions at the same rate of speed, and passing over each other, will form *stationary waves*.   Particles which make up the medium will tend to group themselves into points of much agitation and points of rest.   This phenomenon is called *interference*.   The places of maximum vibration are called *antinodes*.   The places of no vibration are called *nodes*.

The stationary waves which are set up by any musical sound may be represented as follows:

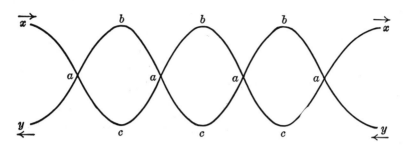

The points *a* represent the nodes, and the points *b* and *c* represent the antinodes. If a small pan containing sand is gently lowered into one end of an open organ pipe while it is sounding, it may be observed that in the middle of the pipe the sand will not be disturbed but that at either end of the pipe the sand will be agitated. From this experiment it may be assumed that each end of an open pipe is an antinode and that the middle of the open pipe is the node. Now, the longest wavelength that can be accommodated in an open organ pipe will contain a node in the middle and two antinodes, one at either end. Under these conditions, the open pipe can accommodate one-half a sound wave. From this observation, the wavelength of an open pipe will be twice the length of the pipe.

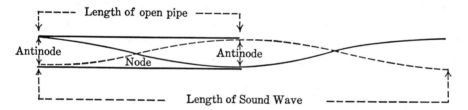

The *wavelength* of the sound produced by a closed pipe is *four times the length of the pipe*. In the closed pipe the node will be at the closed end and the antinode will be at the open end. From this observation, the largest portion of the stationary wave containing a node and an antinode will be one-fourth of the wave; therefore, the sound wave produced by a closed organ pipe will be four times the length of the closed pipe.

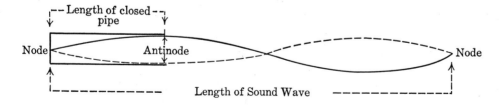

FREQUENCIES USED IN MUSIC

The piano contains most of the practical frequencies used by the musician. The lowest tone on the piano has a frequency of 27.5 vibrations per second, and its highest tone has 4186 vibrations per second. Just as it is necessary to have standards for determining length, mass, and duration, it is necessary for the physicist and the musician to have a standard frequency from which other frequencies may be derived. Efforts to this effect were begun by Mersenne during the 17th century, but it was not until May, 1939, at the International Conference on Pitch, held at London, that $a^1 = 440$ vibrations per second was unanimously adopted as the Standard Pitch.

The first step in locating pitches is to strike any white key in the middle of the piano keyboard and move to the right or left on the white keys, playing them in order. If this experiment is carried out in each direction to the limits of the keyboard, one will observe that frequencies will be heard which seem to repeat the original ones; only they seem to be higher or lower. This phenomenon divides the frequencies into groups which are called *octaves*. The octave pitch has a frequency either twice or one-half that of the given pitch. For example, an octave pitch higher or lower than a given pitch of 440 will be, respectively, a pitch of 880 or 220.

To give a name to each octave, it is necessary to refer to the musician's musical alphabet, which is composed of seven letters, namely, a, b, c, d, e, f, and g. The physicist names the octaves, beginning on c; and the basic letter names of the frequencies in each octave will be c, d, e, f, g, a, and b. The next c will become the fundamental pitch for naming the frequencies in that octave, and so on. The names of the octaves found in musical compositions are as follows:

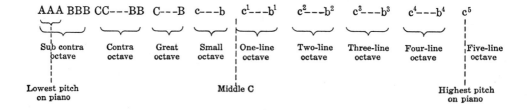

Each octave, however, contains twelve pitches. Each pitch is equidistant from the pitches on either side. This system of tuning was well known by the middle of the 18th century and is called *Equal Temperament*.

The interval resulting on either side of a given pitch is called a *half-tone* or *half-step* and is $\frac{1}{12}$ of an octave. Accordingly, an interval of two half-tones on either side of a given pitch is called a *tone* or *step*, and it is $\frac{1}{6}$ of an octave. The tempered octave contains twelve half-steps or six whole steps. The musician locates any one of the pitches in an octave by using seven letters, namely, a, b, c, d, e, f, and g. The whole-step interval appears between a-b, c-d, d-e, f-g, and g-a. To obtain the remaining pitches, the musician uses a symbol (an *accidental*) in connection with a letter. The *sharp* (♯) used in connection with a letter will obtain a pitch a half-step higher; likewise, the *flat* (♭) used in connection with a letter will obtain a pitch a half-step lower. Accordingly, a *double-sharp* (×) or a *double-flat* (♭♭) will correspondingly raise or lower a given letter a whole step. The *natural* (♮) is used to nullify the sharp or flat.

The following diagram illustrates the location of any desired pitch at the keyboard in the one-line octave:

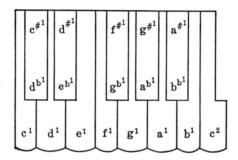

As soon as you have learned the arrangement of the pitches as they are located in the above keyboard, the next step is to find this octave at the piano. Place the text in the middle of the music rack on the piano and sit as nearly in front of the center of the keyboard as possible. With your right hand count five c's from the top of the piano. The fifth c will be middle-c or one-line c (c^1). The octave keyboard diagram in the text corresponds to the octave at the keyboard which you have just found. As soon as you can locate any of the pitches in the c^1 octave, practise locating pitches in the octaves above and below the c^1 octave. You should locate all pitches in the c^1, c^2, etc., octaves with the right hand, and likewise all pitches in the octaves to the left of c^1 with the left hand. You should not move away from c^1 when the pitches are at the extremes of the keyboard. Try to associate the name of the pitch name with its sound and the physical reaction registered while playing it.

EXERCISE 1. Name and play at the piano the following tones:

C, g♯³, e♭¹, DD, f⁴, AAA♯, g²
a, E♭, f♯², c¹, b⁴, GG♭, b♭, d♯³.

Practise this exercise, using other pitch names, until you can locate any pitch at the keyboard.

EXERCISE 2. Identify the octave to which a tone being played belongs. The instructor plays tones (preferably f's, g's, a's) in various octaves, and the student identifies the octave (not actual name of note).

NOTATION OF RELATIVE PITCH

The method of expressing sound in writing used by musicians is called *diaste-matic* (notation by interval). This method uses horizontal lines and symbols (notes) which are placed on the lines or spaces between the lines. The practice of placing at the beginning of a line a letter name to indicate its pitch is credited to Guido d'Arezzo in the 11th century. From this early practice, the clef signs developed to a point in the 17th century where three clef signs were in common use. These signs represent the pitches f, c¹, and g¹. The following table shows the clefs in use:

Pitch	*Symbol*	*Classification*
f	𝄢	F-clef
c¹	𝄡	C-clef
g¹	𝄞	G-clef

The *Great Staff* is composed of eleven lines and ten spaces. It is a theoretical staff (not used), but it includes all the lines and spaces which were in use up to the 18th century. The pitch range of the Great Staff is as follows:

The *staff* used today has five lines and the clef sign to indicate the pitches of the lines and spaces. The name of a clef depends upon its pitch range. Turn to p. 2 of *Sight-Singing Manual*, McHose-Tibbs. You should learn the seven clefs.

INTENSITY

The amount of energy applied to the generator of a sound will affect its loud-ness. In the following figure the solid curved line represents the sound wave of a frequency produced by applying very little energy at its source; the dotted line represents the sound wave of the same frequency produced by applying considerable energy at its source.

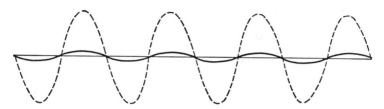

Sound waves which have deep troughs and high crests indicate that a large amount of energy was applied in producing the sound. The sense of sound's being soft or loud is called *intensity*, and its effect on the sound wave is called *amplitude*. In general, the amount of energy applied to a generator of a frequency will not alter the pitch. *Pitch* and *intensity* are independent factors; the former depends on frequency, and the latter upon amplitude.

The musician can control the intensity of musical instruments by less or more energy in bowing, breathing, or striking. In musical notation, the following table illustrates the signs of relative intensity:

Sign	Word	Meaning
pp	pianissimo	very soft
p	piano	soft
mf	mezzo forte	moderately loud
f	forte	loud
ff	fortissimo	very loud
<	crescendo	increasing gradually in intensity
>	{ decrescendo { diminuendo	diminishing gradually in intensity

Dynamic accentuation is another application of the principles of intensity. Composers indicate special intensity in notation as follows:

Sign	Word	Meaning
>̇	accent	emphasize
‾	marcato	emphasize
fz	forzato	forced
sf or sfz	sforzato	forced

TIMBRE OR QUALITY

Quality, the third characteristic of sound, makes it possible for us to distinguish between various vibrating bodies, considering the factors of pitch and intensity as constant.   Thus far, pitch is dependent upon frequency; intensity is dependent upon amplitude.   Quality is found to be based upon the *shape of the wave*.   The wave of a pure tone is as follows:

The wave of a specific musical instrument might take the following shape:

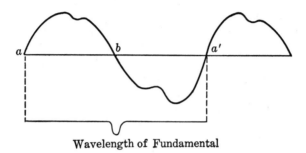

Wavelength of Fundamental

Here the wavelength of the fundamental frequency is aba'.   The shape of the wave, according to the physicists, is determined by the presence of other frequencies varying in their respective intensities.   A sound wave of this type is called a *composite wave*.   The basis for the study of quality is found in the theory of the vibrating string.   The following example illustrates some of the frequencies produced by a string whose fundamental frequency is D:*

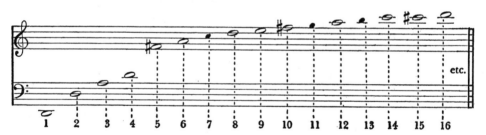

When a string vibrates, it vibrates not only as a whole, but also in two parts, three parts, four parts, and so on.   The frequencies produced by a string as it vibrates as a whole and at the same time in parts are called *partials*.   In the illustration above, Great D is the fundamental and is known as the first partial. The remaining frequencies, beginning with Small d (known as the second partial), are called upper partials.   If the frequency of an upper partial is an exact multiple of the fundamental, it is called a harmonic.   A group of frequencies which are multiples (2, 3, 4, 5, 6, etc.) of a fundamental frequency is known as a harmonic series.

G. S. Ohm and Hermann von Helmholtz are the two principal figures who contributed to the theory of quality.   Ohm discovered that tones produced on

* The frequencies produced by the 7th, 11th, and 13th partials in black notes are out of tune.

musical instruments are composite; that is, not only is the fundamental present, but also other tones of higher frequencies are present. Helmholtz established the law that differences in quality of tones depends solely on the presence and intensity of partials. Contemporary scientific equipment, such as the cathode-ray oscillograph and wave analyzer, confirms the findings of Ohm and Helmholtz. They have made it possible for us to obtain photographs of the sound waves produced by every musical instrument as well as the human voice. In addition, the wave analyzer can determine the presence or absence of partials as well as the amplitude of the partials present.

For complete information on quality, which includes photographs of sound waves and relative harmonic content of the tones produced by various musical instruments, turn to the following authoritative volumes:

CULVER, C. A., *Musical Acoustics* (Philadelphia, The Blakiston Co., 1941).
JEANS, SIR JAMES, *Science and Music* (New York, The Macmillan Co., 1937).
LLOYD, U. S., *Music and Sound* (London, Oxford University Press, 1937).

QUESTIONS

1. Differentiate between a transverse wave and a longitudinal wave.
2. What is meant by the term *wavelength?*
3. Name some musical instruments which produce sound by (*a*) transverse vibration, and (*b*) longitudinal vibration.
4. Describe the transmission of sound from a vibrating source to the ear.
5. Describe the manner in which sound waves may be reflected.
6. Explain sympathetic vibrations.
7. What are forced vibrations?
8. Define the term *resonance.*
9. How does the physicist differentiate between noise and a musical sound?
10. Name the three distinguishing characteristics of a musical sound. Explain each.
11. What are the laws governing vibrating strings?
12. Define a node and an antinode.
13. Explain interference.
14. What are stationary waves?
15. Discuss the laws governing vibrating air columns.
16. Name the octaves.
17. What is equal temperament?
18. What does "$a^1 = 440$" represent?
19. Define the term *diastematic.*
20. How many clef signs are in use?
21. Place on staff paper, for any fundamental pitch, the "harmonic series."
22. What is a composite wave?

ESSAY ASSIGNMENT

The student should write a brief essay on "The Structure of the Human Ear."

The student should write a brief essay on the production of sound on the instrument which is his applied music major.

Part 1

The Elements of Time and Rhythm

Chapter 1

The Beat

Although both the physicist and the musician are concerned with the three characteristics of sound, namely, pitch, intensity, and quality, the musician adds *duration* as a fourth characteristic. Duration is the period of time during which sound or silence lasts. Now this period of time may be very short, short, moderately long, or long. Most of the sounds and silences heard in musical compositions are varying short intervals of time.

The question arises as to how the musician accurately measures durations of tones and silences. The physicist measures the pitch of a sound, the frequencies of different light waves, rays, etc., by a unit of time. This unit is a second. The musician is likewise able to measure the duration of each sound or silence in a musical composition. His unit of time is called a *beat*. Unlike the second, the beat may vary in duration for different musical compositions, or within the same composition. The beat in music is usually a shorter time interval than a second.

THE NATURE OF THE BEAT

Many people react to music by revealing simple movements of the body. These movements occur at regular intervals of time. In the majority of instances, it is found that one can easily walk by keeping step with these simple bodily movements. A natural walking gait established while listening to music becomes one of the best methods for determining the beat. The beat varies for different musical compositions from a slow walking pace to a fast walking pace. The Italians use the word *Tempo* (plural, *Tempi*) to describe the character of the flow of the music. A beat of a short interval of time produces a fast tempo; likewise, a beat of long duration produces a slow tempo.

EXERCISE 1. Recognition of the *beat*.
>Folk songs or suitable compositions will be played, and the student will respond to the music by tapping the beat.

THE SIMPLE BEAT AND THE COMPOUND BEAT

When two compositions using the same time duration for the beat are played one after the other, the character of the beat in the first composition may be quite different from the character of the beat in the second composition. Listen carefully to the character of the beat in each of the following melodies as they are played:

In *The Three Ravens*, the beat is divided into two equal pulsations. While the instructor plays the example a second time, tap the beat with the right hand and tap two equal pulsations with the left hand. You will observe that some sounds will coincide with pulsations, others will appear between the pulsations, and still other sounds will include a number of pulsations. All the different durations are, however, mathematically related to the beat containing two equal divisions.

In *The Lincolnshire Poacher*, the beat is divided into three equal pulsations. As in the first example, tap the beat with the right hand and, at the same time, tap three equal pulsations with the left hand. You will experience durations that are mathematically related to the beat containing three equal divisions.

Most of the music written during the 18th and 19th centuries uses a beat which is basically divisible by two or three. These fundamental pulsations which are felt within the beat are called the *background*.

A beat which has a background of two equal pulsations is a *simple beat*.

A beat which has a background of three equal pulsations is a *compound beat*.

EXERCISE 2. Recognition of the *simple beat* and the *compound beat*.
    a. Folksongs or suitable compositions will be played. The student should respond to the music by tapping the beat with the right hand and the basic division of the beat with the left hand.

b. Folksongs or suitable music will be played. The student should identify the type of beat by reciting or in writing.

NOTATION

Notation in music is a method of indicating relative frequency, silence, duration, intensity, and, at times, timbre. In this chapter, we are concerned with notating duration. The unit of notation is the whole note—𝅝. Its mathematical value is 1. During the 17th century, musicians selected mathematical values less than 1 to represent the beat. Furthermore, it became necessary to devise a simple method of notating compositions which employed a compound beat. The following tables represent the two systems of notation adopted by the early 18th century, and they are to be memorized:

Simple Notation

Note	Value	Rest	Name
𝅜	2	𝄺	Double whole-note
𝅝	1	𝄻	Whole-note
𝅗𝅥	$\frac{1}{2}$	𝄼	Half-note
𝅘𝅥	$\frac{1}{4}$	𝄽 or 𝄽	Quarter-note
𝅘𝅥𝅮	$\frac{1}{8}$	𝄾	Eighth-note
𝅘𝅥𝅯	$\frac{1}{16}$	𝄿	Sixteenth-note
𝅘𝅥𝅰	$\frac{1}{32}$	𝅀	Thirty-second note
𝅘𝅥𝅱	$\frac{1}{64}$	𝅁	Sixty-fourth note

Compound Notation

Note	Value	Rest	Name
𝅝.	$\frac{3}{2}$	𝄻.	Three-halves note
𝅗𝅥.	$\frac{3}{4}$	𝄼.	Three-quarters note
𝅘𝅥.	$\frac{3}{8}$	𝄽. or 𝄽𝄾	Three-eighths note
𝅘𝅥𝅮.	$\frac{3}{16}$	𝄾.	Three-sixteenths note
𝅘𝅥𝅯.	$\frac{3}{32}$	𝄿.	Three thirty-seconds note
𝅘𝅥𝅰.	$\frac{3}{64}$	𝅀.	Three sixty-fourths note
𝅘𝅥𝅱.	$\frac{3}{128}$	𝅁.	Three one-hundred and twenty-eighths note

Chapter 2

Meter

Man seems to possess instinctively the desire to group separate impressions into larger units, especially those received through the visual and auditory sensory organs. In the last chapter, the feeling for the type of beat established the most elementary grouping, namely, equal time durations. The *sense of rhythm* is a natural aptitude for grouping repeated sounds and silences. Although the term *rhythm* may be applied to a variety of musical situations, we are primarily interested at this point in its application to a further use of the beat.

Establishing a M.M. (Maelzel's Metronome) = 72 and keeping the intensity constant, you are to tap the following example:

Now repeat the above example, keeping the M.M. = 72, and accent every other quarter-note.

The mind immediately established a grouping of two beats. Grouping a like number of beats expressed as a rhythm produces *meter*. For the present, we will be concerned with meters which group two, three, or four beats. When the meter of a musical composition uses a grouping of two beats, the composition is said to be in *duple meter*. The following table illustrates the common meters:

Measure	*Name of Meter*
two beats	duple meter
three beats	triple meter
four beats	quadruple meter

22

Each metrical grouping is called a *measure* or *bar*. In notation, these groupings are indicated by a vertical line called a *bar-line*.

The complete explanation of meter requires one more factor. The type of beat which is to be used in the measure is of paramount importance. Compare the rhythmic feeling of the music examples in Chapter 1 as they are played. Although the time duration for the beat is exactly the same for both melodies and the meter is the same, the two melodies are rhythmically quite different. This difference is caused by the background of the beat. Meter must be concerned with grouping of beats as well as with the character of the beat. The first melody uses a simple beat, and the grouping of the beats is duple. This rhythmic feeling is defined as simple duple meter. The second melody is in compound duple meter.

The following table lists the most frequent meters used during the 18th and 19th centuries:

Grouping of Beats	Type of Beat	Name of Meter
2	simple	simple duple
2	compound	compound duple
3	simple	simple triple
3	compound	compound triple
4	simple	simple quadruple
4	compound	compound quadruple

Since the beat is one of a series in a group, the musician assigns the beat a number according to its position. For example, in duple meter, the names of the beats are first beat and second beat.

From a standpoint of rhythm, not all the beats in a measure are found to be of equal importance. The relative importance of the beats in a duple measure is:

1. The first beat is heavy.
2. The second beat is light.

A duple measure may be illustrated graphically as follows:

$$1 \; 2 \mid 1 \; 2 \mid$$

The relative importance of beats in a triple measure is as follows:

1. The first beat is heavy.
2. The second beat is less heavy.
3. The third beat is light.

A triple measure may be illustrated graphically as follows:

$$1 \; 2 \; 3 \mid 1 \; 2 \; 3 \mid$$

The relative importance of beats in a quadruple measure is as follows:

1. The first beat is heavy.
2. The second beat is light.
3. The third beat is less heavy than the first
   but not so light as the second beat.
4. The fourth beat is the lightest beat.

The quadruple bar may be illustrated graphically as follows:

$$1 \; 2 \; 3 \; 4 \mid 1 \; 2 \; 3 \; 4 \mid$$

CONDUCTOR'S BEAT

Although information concerning the history of conducting is somewhat meager as to the methods used in giving instructions to a large group of musicians while they were playing a musical composition, the conductor's beat as we know it today was definitely established during the last half of the 19th century.* The conductor's beat reveals by the movement of the right forearm, with or without a baton, the relative importance of the beats which make up the measure.

The first beat of any measure is a heavy beat, and this is represented by a downward motion of the right forearm.

Duple meter is composed of a heavy beat (first beat) and a light beat (second beat). Using the right forearm, the motion is down and up.

* See articles on conducting in *Grove's Dictionary; Companion to Music*, Percy Scholes; *Harvard Dictionary*, Willi Apel.

Triple meter is composed of a heavy beat (first beat), a less heavy beat (second beat), and a light beat (third beat). Using primarily the forearm, the motion is down, out, and up. The upward motion should be close to the imaginary line described by the down beat.

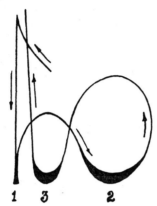

Quadruple meter is composed of a heavy beat (first beat), a light beat (second beat), a less heavy beat (third beat), and a very light beat (fourth beat). Using primarily the forearm, the motion is down, in, out, and up. As in the case of duple and triple meter, the up beat should be in about the same position.

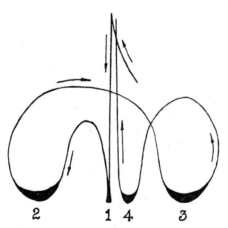

EXERCISE 1. Be able to make the conductor's beat for duple, triple, and quadruple meter.

As soon as the student can make the conductor's beat with the right arm, he should add tapping the simple or compound background with the left hand.

EXERCISE 2. Be able to create any of the three meters in simple or compound form by making the conductor's beat and tapping the background with the left hand.

EXERCISE 3. The instructor will play folk songs or suitable compositions. The student is to identify meter by making the conductor's beat and tapping the background.

EXERCISE 4. The instructor will play folk songs or suitable compositions. The student may recite or write the name of the meter.

METER SIGNATURE

By the middle of the 18th century, composers selected the following symbols of notation to represent the beat:

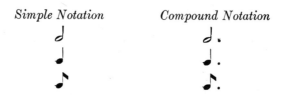

The following table shows the possible meter signatures when using the above symbols to represent the beat:

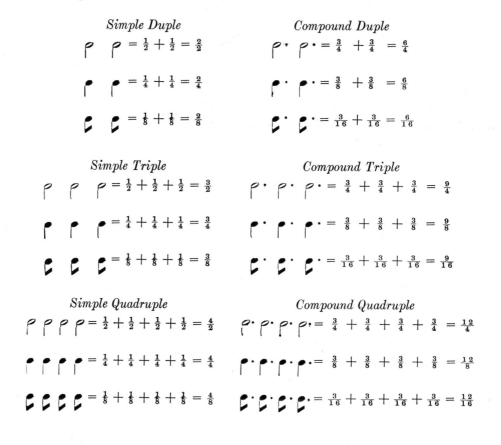

Chapter 3

Elementary Time Durations in Simple Time

THE RHYTHMIC PROBLEM

The beat may be divided into two equal time durations. The notation of these durations, based on the symbols used to represent the beat, are as follows:

Time durations may be made to include two, three, or four beats. This is done by use of the tie. The symbol is in the shape of an arc, namely, . Notations of these durations, based on the symbols used to represent the beat, are:

Beat	Duration of Two Beats	Duration of Three Beats	Duration of Four Beats

Time durations including one beat or a group of beats may extend through the first half of a simple beat.

Beat	Beat Tied into Simple Beat	Two Beats into the Simple Beat	Three Beats into the Simple Beat

27

RHYTHMIC READING

Rhythmic reading is a special drill in which the student reproduces at sight only the durations represented by the symbols in printed music. This is made possible by reciting a series of syllables known as rhythmic syllables. Since the beat is the fundamental unit of time in the period of music which we are studying, it is given the unit numbers, such as 1, 2, 3, etc. In the previous chapter, it was shown that each beat was assigned a number depending upon its position in the measure. These numbers are the fundamental rhythmic syllables for the beat and are explained in the *Sight-Singing Manual*, p. 6.

The rhythmic syllables for the simple division of the beat are one-te (pronounced *tay*). See *Sight-Singing Manual*, p. 6.

The object in rhythmic reading is not only to develop at sight an accurate conception of the rhythmic organization of a musical composition, but also to develop the ability to reproduce this rhythmic organization. The student should make the conductor's beat with the right arm, tap the background with the left hand, and recite the rhythmic syllables. This drill should be continued until he understands the rhythmic problems of this chapter.

The rhythmic reading drills may be conducted in the following manner:

1. Class as a whole performs the rhythmic reading. Either the teacher or a member of the class may direct the drill.
2. A member of the class performs the rhythmic reading.

The exercises which may be used for rhythmic reading are from No. 1 through No. 110 in Section I of the *Sight-Singing Manual*. Additional exercises may be found in the *Folk Song Sight-Singing Series*,* Book I (1–110), Book II (1–100), and Book III (1–59).

RHYTHMIC DICTATION†

In this presentation of the elements which make up a musical composition, mastery of the problem will be governed by a threefold plan of instruction. This plan is as follows:

1. Presentation of the theory of a problem.
2. Sight reading, including the problem.
3. Dictation, including the problem.

The mastery of rhythmic dictation is the first step in developing the ability to reproduce in notation a musical composition which is being played. Musicians use dictation as one of the ways to test one's knowledge of the elements which make up a musical composition.

---

* London, Oxford University Press (New York, Carl Fischer, Inc.).

† Dictation exercises for Chapter 3 are found in *Teachers Dictation Manual*, Part I, Section I.

INSTRUCTIONS FOR RHYTHMIC DICTATION.

Type 1

You will be given the meter signature of the melody.

    a. The melody will be played twice.
    b. Using the conductor's beat and tapping the background with the left hand, you are to sing the melody on a neutral syllable (*Lah*).
    c. Using the conductor's beat and tapping the background, you are to sing the melody, using the rhythmic syllables.
    d. You are to write the bar lines and notation of the melody on the second line of the staff.
    e. The melody will be played once more for you to check your solution.

Example: The instructor announces that the meter is $\frac{2}{2}$.

    a. The following melody is played twice.

    b. Using the conductor's beat and tapping the background with the left hand, you are to sing the above melody on a neutral syllable.
    c. Using the conductor's beat and tapping the background with the left hand, you are to sing the above melody, using the rhythmic syllables.
    d. You are to write the bar lines and notation of the melody on the second line of the staff, as follows:

    e. The melody will be played once more for you to check your solution.

Type 2

Type 2 is the same as Type 1, with one exception. You will be given the symbol which represents the beat. You will have to determine the meter from the playing of the melody.

Type 3

Type 3 eliminates the steps *b* and *c* of the previous dictation procedures. You will be given either the meter signature or the symbol which represents the beat.

    a. The melody will be played twice.
    b. You are to write the correct notation on the second line of the staff.
    c. The melody will be played once more for you to check your solution.

Chapter 4

Durations within the Compound Beat

THEORY OF THE PROBLEM

The reciting syllables for the compound beat are "one-lah-lee." Turn to the *Sight-Singing Manual*, Section II, page 30, and study the examples. The use of the tie within the compound beat produces unequal time durations. Memorize the following tables:

		Compound	Tie 1st and 2nd	Tie 2nd and 3rd
Rhythmic	*Beat*	*Division*	*Background*	*Background*
Syllables:	one	one - lah - lee	one - lee	one - lah-
Notation:				

A beat may be tied into the compound division of a beat.

		Beat Tied into		Beat Tied into	
Rhythmic	*Beat*	*Compound Division*		*Unequal Durations*	
Syllables:	one	one — lah - lee	one — lee	one — lah

Durations of more than one beat may be tied into the compound beat on the unequal durations within the compound beat. The following table illustrates one of the many possible combinations:

RHYTHMIC READING

The exercises which may be used for rhythmic reading are from No. 111 through No. 130 in Section II of the *Sight-Singing Manual*. Additional exercises may be found in the *Folk Song Sight-Singing* Series, Book IV (78, 80, 82, 84, 86 through 90), Book V (47 through 58, 67, 79, 86), Book VI (67, 77 through 81).

RHYTHMIC DICTATION*

The rhythmic dictation drills will follow the plan of Type 1, Type 2, and Type 3 as found in Chapter 3.

* Rhythmic dictation exercises are found in the *Teachers Dictation Manual*, Part I, Section II.

Chapter 5

Subdivision of the Simple Beat into Four Durations

THE RHYTHMIC PROBLEM

The simple beat may be broken down into four equal time durations. This is made possible by subdividing each background into two equal time durations. The reciting syllables for the simple beat are "one-te." The reciting syllables for the beat divided into four equal durations are "one-ta-te-ta."

The notation for the division of a simple beat into four equal time durations is as follows:

	Beat	Division of Four
Rhythmic Syllables:	one	one ta te ta
Notation:		

Turn to the *Sight-Singing Manual*, Section III, page 36, first score.

Through the use of the tie, the simple beat when divided into four equal pulsations may contain five different unequal durations.

Tying the first and second pulsations will produce	one - te-ta
Tying the second and third pulsations will produce	one ta - ta
Tying the third and fourth pulsations will produce	one ta te -
Tying the first, second, and third pulsations will produce	one - - ta
Tying the second, third, and fourth pulsations will produce	one ta - -

The notation for the unequal time durations is as follows:

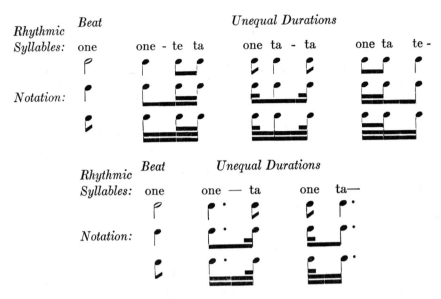

For practical examples of the unequal time durations with the simple beat, turn to the *Sight-Singing Manual*, page 36, second, third, fourth, and fifth scores.

RHYTHMIC READING

The exercises which may be used for rhythmic reading are in the *Sight-Singing Manual*, Section III, No. 131 through No. 179. Additional exercises may be found in the *Folk Song Sight-Singing Series*, Book III (60 through 65), Book IV (1 through 20, 50, 65, 94, 96), Book V (1, 2, 7, 8, 10, 14, 16, 18, 21, 25, 26, 35, 37, 38, 44, 46, 68, 69, 73, 75, 87, 90), Book VII (27 through 35, 61, 65, 68, 82).

RHYTHMIC DICTATION*

The dictation procedure is the same as in former chapters.

* Rhythmic dictation exercises are found in the *Teachers Dictation Manual*, Part I, Section III.

Chapter 6

Further Study of the Tie

THE RHYTHMIC PROBLEM

Although tying a beat into unequal durations within the compound beat has been
presented, this chapter will continue to drill this rhythmic problem and, in addition,
include tying the beat or durations of more than one beat into the unequal durations
within the simple beat. No new reciting syllables are needed for this problem.
The following examples illustrate some of the many possible time durations which
are the result of tying the beat or a number of beats into the unequal time durations:

Rewrite the above example, using the two remaining triple compound meters.

Rewrite the above example, using another simple quadruple meter.

RHYTHMIC READING

The exercises which may be used for rhythmic reading are in the *Sight-Singing Manual*, Section IV (156 through 179). Additional exercises may be found in the *Folk Song Sight-Singing Series*, Book V (10, 52, 54, 79), Book VII (49). This rhythmic problem in a simple meter is quite rare in folk songs.

RHYTHMIC DICTATION*

The dictation procedure is the same as in former chapters.

* Rhythmic dictation exercises are found in the *Teachers Dictation Manual*, Part I, Section IV.

Chapter 7

Syncopation

THE RHYTHMIC PROBLEM

If a duration begins on a light pulsation and extends through a heavy pulsation, the rhythmic effect is called *syncopation*. The light pulsation may be a light beat or a light pulsation within a beat. Thus far, we have generated ties, for the most part, on heavy pulsations. Study the examples found on page 51, Section V, of the *Sight-Singing Manual*. For rhythmic notation transposition, write the examples which you have just studied, using different symbols to represent the beat. For example, rewrite the first example in $\frac{2}{2}$, and then in $\frac{2}{8}$.

RHYTHMIC READING

The exercises which may be used for rhythmic reading are in the *Sight-Singing Manual*, Section V (180 through 206). Additional exercises may be found in the *Folk Song Sight-Singing Series*, Book VI (1 through 17, 49, 50), Book VII (57, 58, 59).

RHYTHMIC DICTATION*

The dictation procedure is the same as in former chapters.

* Rhythmic dictation exercises are found in the *Teachers Dictation Manual*, Part I, Section V.

Chapter 8

Superimposed Backgrounds and Superimposed Meters

THE RHYTHMIC PROBLEM

In the course of a musical composition, durations based upon the compound beat may be introduced in simple meter, or vice versa. When this occurs, it is known as *superimposed backgrounds*. Study carefully the explanation of the Rhythmic Reading, as found on page 59, Section VI, of the *Sight-Singing Manual*.

The following table shows the method of notating durations within a compound beat superimposed on the background of a simple beat.

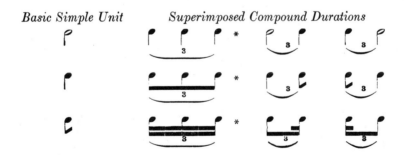

For many years, there have been two schools of thought concerning notating durations based on a simple unit when they are superimposed on a compound beat. The author will not argue this point but will provide the system of notation which has been presented and accepted by composers and authors of musical dictionaries of the last thirty years. One of the most recent books which is used as a basis for the last statement is the *Oxford Companion to Music*, by Percy Scholes, published by the Oxford University Press.

* These durations are called a *triplet*.

The following table shows the method of notating duration within a simple beat superimposed on the background of a compound beat:*

Basic Compound Unit

Superimposed Simple Durations

Occasionally, the duration of an established simple meter may have another simple meter superimposed upon it. Study carefully the explanation of superimposed meter as found on page 59, Section VI, of the *Sight-Singing Manual.*

RHYTHMIC READING

The exercises which may be used for rhythmic reading are in the *Sight-Singing Manual,* Section VI (207 through 217). Additional exercises may be found in the *Folk Song Sight-Singing Series,* Book VII (16 through 20, 66, 72, 74).

RHYTHMIC DICTATION††

The dictation procedure is the same as in former chapters.

*For the notation of frequent backgrounds which are superimposed in simple and compound time, see musical dictionaries under the headings of *quintuplet, sextolet, septolet,* etc. The instructor should make this subject an outside paper assignment.

** These durations are called a *duplet.*

† These durations are called a *quadruplet.*

†† Rhythmic dictation exercises are found in the *Teachers Dictation Manual,* Part I, Section VI.

Chapter 9

Further Study of the Subdivision of the Background

❧

THE RHYTHMIC PROBLEM

The background of the compound beat may be divided into two, three, or four equal durations.

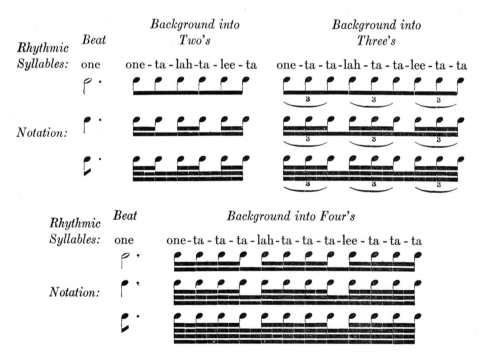

Any of the above equal durations may be converted into unequal durations by the use of the tie. Many of these unequal durations will be syncopations.

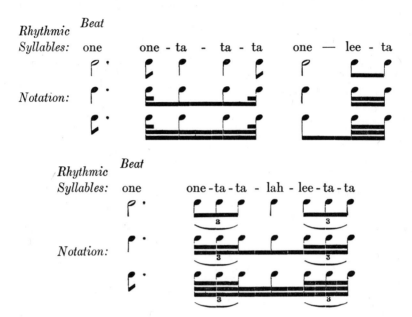

The possible rhythmic groupings are too numerous to list. The student, however, can rely upon the feeling for the beat and its background to produce correctly one of these rhythmic groupings in Rhythmic Reading, or to solve one of these rhythmic groupings in Rhythmic Dictation.

The background of the simple beat may also be divided into two, three, or four equal durations.

Any of the above equal durations may be converted into unequal durations within the beat by the use of the tie. A few of the many possible unequal durations are as follows:

RHYTHMIC READING

To aid the student in perfecting his ability to perform accurately the many rhythmic groupings which subdivision of the beat provides, the following organized rhythmic drills should be practised by tapping the examples, as well as by reciting the rhythmic syllables:

With the above drills well mastered, turn to the *Sight-Singing Manual*, Section VII (218 through 249) for regular practice in Rhythmic Reading. Additional exercises may be found in the *Folk Song Sight-Singing Series*, Book VI (82 through 90), Book VII (36 through 48, 50, 52, 53, 73, 76, 85, 90).

For further practice, the student should study examples of the use of subdivision of the background found in the music literature of his applied field. He should be prepared to tap or recite with rhythmic syllables the examples which he submits.

RHYTHMIC DICTATION*

The dictation procedure is the same as in former chapters.

* Rhythmic dictation exercises are found in the *Teachers Dictation Manual*, Part I, Section VII.

$\mathcal{C}$hapter 10

The Divided Beat

The meter signature does not always indicate the character of the conductor's beat. Tempo indications and the character of a composition strongly influence the manner in which the conductor's beat is utilized. These conditions frequently make it advisable for the conductor to divide each beat in the measure into two or three secondary beats. These secondary beat indications then produce the divided beat.

The conductor's divided beat for a simple duple meter signature is illustrated below.

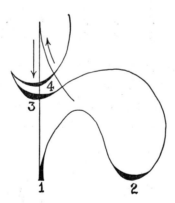

The author has found that musicians count the simple duple divided beat meter signature in one of two ways. One method of counting is "1-and-2-and" which in our rhythmic syllable system is "1-te-2-te"; the other method is to count each motion of the conductor's beat as a beat, namely, "1-2-3-4." The latter method is employed by the conductor when he tells his performers that he plans to conduct the $\frac{2}{4}$ in four.

The conductor's divided beat for the simple triple meter is given below:

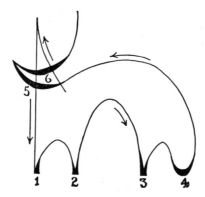

The conductor's divided beat for simple quadruple meter signature is given below.

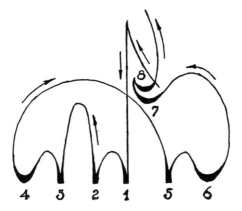

It is important to remember that in the three simple meters just discussed, the divided beat procedure retains the original beat pattern for duple, triple, and quadruple conductor's beat.   This idea is carried out in connection with the conductor's divided beat for the compound meters, which are as follows:

Divided Duple Compound Meter   *Divided Triple Compound Meter*

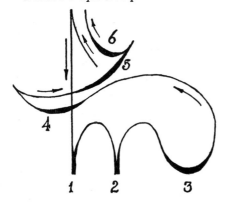
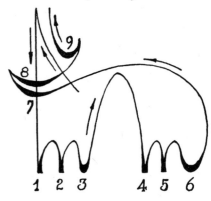

Divided Compound Quadruple Meter

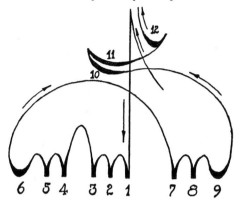

When the divided beat is used, the following rhythmic syllables are used for the beats in the measure:

Simple duple. 1–2–3–4
Simple triple. 1–2–3–4–5–6
Simple quadruple. 1–2–3–4–5–6–7–8
Compound duple. 1–2–3–4–5–6
Compound triple. 1–2–3–4–5–6–7–8–9
Compound quadruple. 1–2–3–4–5–6–7–8–9–10–11–12

Turn to the *Sight-Singing Manual*, page 78, and observe the method of using the rhythmic syllables for the exercises in $\frac{2}{4}$ and $\frac{6}{8}$, respectively.

RHYTHMIC READING

The examples which may be used for rhythmic reading are found in the *Sight-Singing Manual*, Section IX, Exercises 260 through 267. For further drill in rhythmic reading, the student should select music which is in his applied field. He is to bring it to class and recite with rhythmic syllables portions of these compositions which require the divided beat.

No rhythmic dictation will be required in connection with the study of the divided beat.

The divided beat is frequently used to control groups of musicians in the performance of rallentandos, etc. This problem appears in the cadence formula. Since this is not a course in conducting, the author will relegate this study to classes in conducting. It is, however, important for the member of a chorus or orchestra to watch for the use of the divided beat near the close of a section or movement of an extended composition.

$\mathcal{C}$hapter 11

Further Study of Meter

Up to this chapter, the study of meter has been confined to the basic duple, triple, and quadruple meters and to the same meters as a basis for the divided beat. In 18th century music, one encounters meters containing one beat, six beats, eight beats, nine beats, and twelve beats. Of these meters, a one-beat meter is the least encountered. Probably the only quintuple (five-beat) meter used in the 18th century is from Georg F. Handel's opera, *Orlando* (1732), in which there appear three measures of $\frac{5}{8}$, then a $\frac{4}{4}$, followed by a $\frac{4}{4}$. The example is as follows:*

* This example is from a thesis from the Graduate School of the Eastman School of Music of the University of Rochester. Marian Wolfe, *Changing Time Signatures*, June, 1939.

In the 19th century, meters containing five beats were established, although they are rare. It is not until the last part of the century that one encounters meters containing seven beats.

SIMPLE SINGLE AND COMPOUND SINGLE

Compound single is more frequent than simple single. In the late 18th century and in the 19th century, scherzos from the symphonies are conducted in one beat to the measure. When this occurs, the meter is compound single.

The conductor's beat for single meter contains the usual downbeat from which the arm bounces back to prepare the next downbeat.

I

The meter signatures for simple single and compound single are given in the following table:

Simple *Single Signature*			*Compound* *Single Signature*		
ρ	$= \frac{1}{2}$	$= \frac{1}{2}$	$\rho \cdot$	$= \frac{3}{4}$	$= \frac{3}{4}$
ρ	$= \frac{1}{4}$	$= \frac{1}{4}$	$\rho \cdot$	$= \frac{3}{8}$	$= \frac{3}{8}$
ρ	$= \frac{1}{8}$	$= \frac{1}{8}$	$\rho \cdot$	$= \frac{3}{16}$	$= \frac{3}{16}$

SIMPLE QUINTUPLE AND COMPOUND QUINTUPLE

The quintuple meter is composed of five beats. These beats are grouped either $2 + 3$ or $3 + 2$. Quintuple meter is usually considered a union of duple and triple meter. Contemporary composers like to consider the five beats as a single grouping. The author, however, finds that practically all the early examples of quintuple meter reveal a tendency to group in sets of 2 and 3, or 3 and 2. Under these circumstances, the conductor's beat follows two patterns, as shown in the following examples.

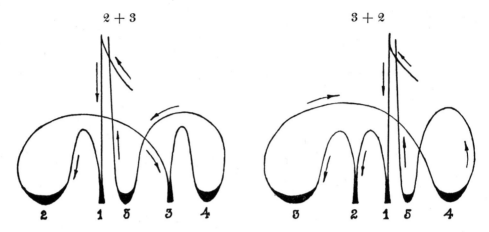

The possible meter signatures for simple quintuple and compound quintuple are given in the following table:

$$\text{Simple Quintuple} \qquad \text{Signature}$$

$$= \tfrac{1}{2} + \tfrac{1}{2} + \tfrac{1}{2} + \tfrac{1}{2} + \tfrac{1}{2} = \tfrac{5}{2}$$

$$= \tfrac{1}{4} + \tfrac{1}{4} + \tfrac{1}{4} + \tfrac{1}{4} + \tfrac{1}{4} = \tfrac{5}{4}$$

$$= \tfrac{1}{8} + \tfrac{1}{8} + \tfrac{1}{8} + \tfrac{1}{8} + \tfrac{1}{8} = \tfrac{5}{8}$$

$$\text{Compound Quintuple} \qquad \text{Signature}$$

$$= \tfrac{3}{4} + \tfrac{3}{4} + \tfrac{3}{4} + \tfrac{3}{4} + \tfrac{3}{4} = \tfrac{15}{4}$$

$$= \tfrac{3}{8} + \tfrac{3}{8} + \tfrac{3}{8} + \tfrac{3}{8} + \tfrac{3}{8} = \tfrac{15}{8}$$

$$= \tfrac{3}{16} + \tfrac{3}{16} + \tfrac{3}{16} + \tfrac{3}{16} + \tfrac{3}{16} = \tfrac{15}{16}$$

SIMPLE SEXTUPLE AND COMPOUND SEXTUPLE

The conductor's beat for simple sextuple and compound sextuple is as follows:

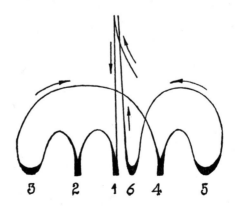

The possible meter signatures for simple sextuple and compound sextuple are as follows:

Simple Sextuple .... *Signature*

$\mathcal{P} \ \mathcal{P} \ \mathcal{P} \ \mathcal{P} \ \mathcal{P} \ \mathcal{P} = \frac{1}{2} + \frac{1}{2} + \frac{1}{2} + \frac{1}{2} + \frac{1}{2} + \frac{1}{2} = \frac{6}{2}$

$\mathcal{P} \ \mathcal{P} \ \mathcal{P} \ \mathcal{P} \ \mathcal{P} \ \mathcal{P} = \frac{1}{4} + \frac{1}{4} + \frac{1}{4} + \frac{1}{4} + \frac{1}{4} + \frac{1}{4} = \frac{6}{4}$

$\mathcal{E} \ \mathcal{E} \ \mathcal{E} \ \mathcal{E} \ \mathcal{E} \ \mathcal{E} = \frac{1}{8} + \frac{1}{8} + \frac{1}{8} + \frac{1}{8} + \frac{1}{8} + \frac{1}{8} = \frac{6}{8}$

Compound Sextuple .... *Signature*

$\mathcal{P.} \ \mathcal{P.} \ \mathcal{P.} \ \mathcal{P.} \ \mathcal{P.} \ \mathcal{P.} = \frac{3}{4} + \frac{3}{4} + \frac{3}{4} + \frac{3}{4} + \frac{3}{4} + \frac{3}{4} = \frac{18}{4}$

$\mathcal{P.} \ \mathcal{P.} \ \mathcal{P.} \ \mathcal{P.} \ \mathcal{P.} \ \mathcal{P.} = \frac{3}{8} + \frac{3}{8} + \frac{3}{8} + \frac{3}{8} + \frac{3}{8} + \frac{3}{8} = \frac{18}{8}$

$\mathcal{E.} \ \mathcal{E.} \ \mathcal{E.} \ \mathcal{E.} \ \mathcal{E.} \ \mathcal{E.} = \frac{3}{16} + \frac{3}{16} + \frac{3}{16} + \frac{3}{16} + \frac{3}{16} + \frac{3}{16} = \frac{18}{16}$

SIMPLE SEPTUPLE AND COMPOUND SEPTUPLE

In the last quarter of the 19th century, one occasionally encounters in editions of folk music, especially from Russia, and music by Russian and French composers, excellent examples of septuple meter. A septuple meter is usually divided into two groupings of the beats within the measure. These groupings are either 3 + 4 or 4 + 3. In a sense, septuple meter is considered a union of triple and quadruple meters. The conductor's beat follows two patterns, as shown in the examples:

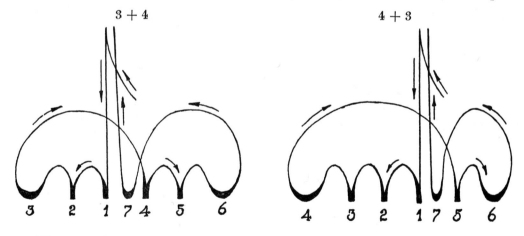

3 + 4 ...... 4 + 3

The possible meter signatures for simple septuple and compound septuple are as follows:

Simple Septuple ...... *Signature*

$\mathcal{P} \ \mathcal{P} \ \mathcal{P} \ \mathcal{P} \ \mathcal{P} \ \mathcal{P} \ \mathcal{P} = \frac{1}{2} \times 7 = \frac{7}{2}$

$\mathcal{P} \ \mathcal{P} \ \mathcal{P} \ \mathcal{P} \ \mathcal{P} \ \mathcal{P} \ \mathcal{P} = \frac{1}{4} \times 7 = \frac{7}{4}$

$\mathcal{E} \ \mathcal{E} \ \mathcal{E} \ \mathcal{E} \ \mathcal{E} \ \mathcal{E} \ \mathcal{E} = \frac{1}{8} \times 7 = \frac{7}{8}$

Compound Septuple   *Signature*

$$\text{♩. ♩. ♩. ♩. ♩. ♩. ♩.} = \tfrac{3}{4} \times 7 = \tfrac{21}{4}$$

$$\text{♪. ♪. ♪. ♪. ♪. ♪. ♪.} = \tfrac{3}{8} \times 7 = \tfrac{21}{8}$$

$$\text{♬. ♬. ♬. ♬. ♬. ♬. ♬.} = \tfrac{3}{16} \times 7 = \tfrac{21}{16}$$

Meters containing eight, nine, and twelve beats use the conductor's beat designs outlined in the lesson on the divided beat. The possible meter signatures for eight (octuple), nine (nonuple), and twelve (duodecuple), based on a quarter-note in simple meter and a three-eighths-note in compound meter, are as follows:

	Simple			*Compound*	
	Beat		*Signature*	*Beat*	*Signature*
Octuple	♩	$= \tfrac{1}{4} \times$	$8 = \tfrac{8}{4}$	♩.	$= \tfrac{3}{8} \times \quad 8 = \tfrac{24}{8}$
Nonuple	♩	$= \tfrac{1}{4} \times$	$9 = \tfrac{9}{4}$	♩.	$= \tfrac{3}{8} \times \quad 9 = \tfrac{27}{8}$
Duodecuple	♩	$= \tfrac{1}{4} \times$	$12 = \tfrac{12}{4}$	♩.	$= \tfrac{3}{8} \times 12 = \tfrac{36}{8}$

RHYTHMIC READING

Examples for rhythmic reading are found in the *Sight-Singing Manual*, Section XI, No. 310 through No. 319. Further examples may be found in the *Folk Song Sight-Singing Series*, Book VII, No. 6, 7, 8, and 9.

RHYTHMIC DICTATION

Collections of Russian and English folksongs will contain suitable dictation exercises using quintuple and septuple meters. The method of taking dictation will be the same as in former chapters.*

* At this stage of the student's advancement, the material presented in this chapter should be combined with melodic dictation.

Chapter 12

Mixed Meter, Poly-Meter, Unusual Meters

MIXED METERS

The term *mixed meter* is applied to different meters which follow each other in close succession. The resulting measures are of different time durations. When mixed meter appears in the course of a composition, the durations in the measures involved are usually controlled by the following circumstances:

1. The beat of the first measure, as the unifying duration, equals the beat of the second measure.
2. The background of the beat of the first measure as the unifying duration becomes the beat of the second measure; or, the beat of the first measure as the unifying duration becomes the background of the second measure.

The selection of the conductor's beat for the measures involved in mixed meter will be determined by the unifying duration.

Although the use of mixed meter is usually attributed to the 20th century composers, occasional examples appear as early as the late 17th century. The following aria from Georg Friedrich Handel's opera *Rinaldo* (1717) has mixed meter as an integral part.

In performing this portion of the aria, the eighth note becomes the unifying duration as the switch takes place from the 3/8 to the 2/4.   The rhythmic reading syllables and the conductor's beat are given directly below the example.

The next example shows how a ritard may be accomplished in a cadence formual through the use of mixed meter.   The duration of the beat (quarter note) becomes the unifying element when the switch from 3/4 to 3/2 takes place.

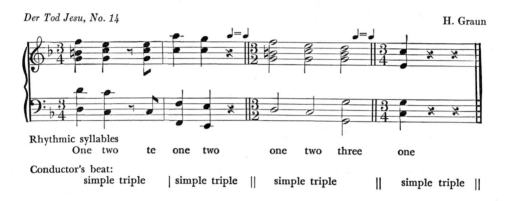

Der Tod Jesu, No. 14   H. Graun

Rhythmic syllables
     One two   te   one two   one   two   three   one

Conductor's beat:
         simple triple | simple triple || simple triple || simple triple ||

In the following example, the duration of the quarter note (the beat) remains the same when the switch from the 3/4 to the 4/4 takes place:

Papillion, Op. 2, No. 11   R. Schumann

Rhythmic syllables for melody:
     One te   two te three te   one ta te two te three ta te four - te

Conductor's beat:
     Simple triple   simple quadruple

     one   te ta two te ta   three

simple triple

RHYTHMIC READING

The exercises which may be used for rhythmic reading are in the *Sight-Singing Manual*, Section XI, No. 320 through 348, and 350. Additional exercises are available in the *Folk Song Sight-Singing Series*, Book VII, No. 10 through 15, and 88.

RHYTHMIC DICTATION

Suitable dictation exercises may be found in collections of English, Russian, and French folksongs. The dictation procedure is the same as in former chapters.

POLY-METER

The term *poly-meter* means the simultaneous use of more than one type of meter. The following 18th century harpsichord composition has the right hand performing compound triple and, at the same time, the left hand performing simple triple:

Pieces de clavecin, Book II (1716)   F. Couperin

Although poly-meter is a device not often used before 1900, compositions containing it are found in the 18th and 19th centuries. Illustrations of the use of poly-meter may be found in the following list of composers:

ANDRE, Anton (1775)	*Quartet, opus 54.*	2/4, 3/4, and 4/4 in different instruments.
BRAHMS, Johannes (1876)	*Quartet, opus 67.*	2/4 and 6/8
(1892)	*Trio, opus 114.*	6/8 in two parts and 2/4 in piano for two measures.

CHAUSSON, Ernest
    (1891)   *Symphony I*, second movement.   12/8 and 4/4.

GOUNOD, Charles
    (1859)   *Faust*, Prelude to Act IV.   12/8 in flute and clarinet against 4/4 in remainder of score.

GRIEG, Edward
    (1879)   *Quartet, opus 27.*   2/4 and 6/8.
    (1891)   *Quartet in F minor.*   2/4 and 6/8 in viola.

MOZART, Wolfgang   "Don Giovanni" Finale of Act I   Minuet, Contretanz, and Waltz

TSCHAIKOWSKY, Peter I
    (1878)   *Symphony IV*, first movement.   9/8 and 3/4.
                                    Symphony VI, third movement.   12/8 and 4/4.

UNUSUAL METER

By the use of the term *unusual meter*, one classifies any meter which is not included in the previous discussion. Unusual meter is found in 20th century music. The author will present a list of references which will illustrate unusual meter. $\frac{4+2+3}{8}$ is a meter signature which appears in Bela Bartok's String Quartet No. V. He uses this signature to reveal clearly to the player how he divided the measure. He does not want the feeling of 9/8. See measure eight and nine of the Scherzo. In measure sixty-seven of the same movement, the signature is $\frac{3+2+2+3}{8}$.

$2\frac{2}{3}$ appears in Florent Schmitt's piano composition, Ombres, opus 64. See measure 125. You will find that neither 3/4 nor 9/8 adequately explains the grouping. The measure is actually a poly-meter. In measure ninety-eight of the same composition $\frac{3\frac{1}{2}}{4}$ meter appears. $\frac{5\frac{1}{2}}{4}$ appears in Charles Ives' *Holiday Symphony*, first movement. The grouping in the measure is as follows:

$\frac{4\frac{1}{2}}{4}$ appears in Ives' Symphony IV in the second movement. The grouping in the measure is as follows:

In the two examples of Charles Ives, the quarter note is the basic beat for the measure. Each measure, however, is lengthened by the addition of an eighth note which happens to be the duration of the simple background.

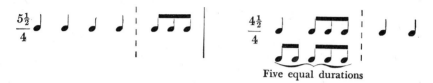

Five equal durations

Carlos Chávez introduces a measure containing an eighth note, and the signature selected is $\frac{1}{12}$. This signature appears in the third movement of his *Sonata for Piano*. This meter signature appears in a succession of mixed meter.

According to the character of the music at this place, Chávez believes that it is more practical to introduce a measure having a duration of one-twelfth the value of the preceding measure than to combine the last two measures, using a meter signature $\frac{13}{8}$.

To complete the picture of experiments by composers, this discussion would not be complete without mentioning the fact that during the past sixty years compositions have appeared which lack meter signatures. The French composer, Eric Satie, was one of the first to discard the meter signature. Some compositions which do not have meter signatures are:

TANSMAN, Alexandre. *Trois Préludes en Forme de Blues* (Piano Solo)
TOCH, Ernest. *Three Piano Pieces*, Opus 32
PALMGREN, Selim. *Opus 17, No. 19—Vogelsang* (Solo Piano Piece)
SATIE, Erik. *Descriptions Automatiques* (3 Piano Pieces)
MOMPOU, Federico. *Fêtes Lointaines* (6 Piano Pieces)
KOECHLIN, Charles. *Douze Petites Pièces, Opus 41* (12 Piano Pieces)
MESSIAEN, Olivier. *Combat de la Mort et de la Vie* (Organ Composition)

* This group of eighth notes is not a triplet.

Part 2

The Tonal Elements

Chapter 13

Intervals

The musician must turn to the physicist for an accurate definition of the interval. A *musical interval* is the relation between two tones, expressed as a ratio of their frequencies. For example, two tones whose frequencies are 80 and 40 (2:1 or 2/1) create the octave, and the interval produced by two tones whose frequencies are 880 and 440 (2:1 or 2/1) is also an octave. As long as the frequencies of the components involved can be reduced to the ratio 2:1, the interval will be an octave. In the following example, the ear of the musician identifies each interval as an octave; yet the frequencies used for each example are quite different:

587.4	1046.4	415.4	1244.6	138.6	349.2
293.7	523.2	207.7	622.3	69.3	174.6

Keeping this in mind, it is important to consider the fact that in music there are relatively few intervals in use. These intervals are divided into two classifications: *consonant* and *dissonant*. A *consonant interval* is one whose ratio of the frequencies can be expressed by small numbers and whose aural effect is pleasing. A *dissonant interval* is one whose ratio of the frequencies can be expressed in large numbers and whose aural effect is unpleasant.*

---

* Hermann von Helmholtz (1821–1894) and later Rudolph Koenig (1832–1901) and other acoustical investigators show that these unpleasant aural effects are caused by beats of the upper partials as they disturb the united sound. Those who wish to study this point in detail should turn to the following texts:

CULVER, CHARLES A., *Musical Acoustics* (Philadelphia, The Blakiston Company).
LLOYD, L. S., *Music and Sound* (London, Oxford University Press, 1937).

The student should bear in mind that the musician through the ages has changed his mind concerning dissonance and consonance. In this text the matter of consonance and dissonance will be limited to the 18th and 19th century interpretation.

The fundamental consonant intervals of just intonation employed in the art of music are as follows:

	Name of Interval	*Ratio of Frequencies*
	Perfect Unison	1/1
	Perfect Octave	2/1
Perfect Consonances	Perfect Fifth	3/2
	Perfect Fourth	4/3
Imperfect Consonances*	Major Third	5/4
	Minor Third	6/5

In equal temperament tuning, the only intervals which are in tune with just intonation are the perfect unison and the perfect octave. The remaining intervals are slightly larger or smaller as the case may be; consequently, they will be out of tune to the extent of a few beats in relation to just intonation. Under ordinary conditions of musical performance the musician accepts this slight out-of-tune variance with just intonation.

PLAYING AND WRITING THE FUNDAMENTAL INTERVALS

The component tones of the perfect unison have the same spelling. The perfect unison is placed on the staff in the following ways:

EXERCISE 1. Write the perfect unison for each of the following notes:

The component tones of the perfect octave have the same spelling. The perfect octave is placed on the staff in the following manner:

---

* The imperfect consonances of the major sixth and minor sixth will be presented in Chapter 16.

EXERCISE 2.* Write the second note a perfect octave above the given note.

EXERCISE 3.* Write the second note a perfect octave below the given note.

EXERCISE 4. Play a perfect octave placing the second note above the given note.

Use right hand   Use left hand

EXERCISE 5. Play a perfect octave placing the second note below the given note.

Use right hand   Use left hand

The tempered perfect fifth contains seven tempered half-tones and it is slightly smaller than the just perfect fifth. In order to locate the interval of a fifth, one must turn to the musical alphabet. A fifth may be obtained by counting five letters upwards or downwards. For example:

the fifth above a is as follows: the fifth below a is as follows:

e	5		a	5
d	4		g	4
c	3		f	3
b	2		e	2
a	1		d	1

In equal temperament tuning, the component tones of the perfect fifth have the same accidental, with the exception of the perfect fifth built on b: c to g; d♭ to a♭; f♯ to c♯; e♯ to b♯; etc. Since the fifth from b to f in the musical alphabet contains only six half-tones, the f must be raised one half-tone. The perfect fifths involving b to f will be spelled b♭ to f and b to f♯.

---

* These exercises provide practice in the writing of music manuscript. The instructor should not permit the student to write the notes carelessly.

EXERCISE 6. Give the spelling of the tone a perfect fifth above the following tones: f; g♯; c♭; e♯; b; a♯; e♭; f♭; d♯.

Give the spelling of the tone a perfect fifth below the following tones: f♯; a; c♭; d; d♯; b; g♭; a♯; f; e♭.

To locate the interval of the fifth on the staff, the second note will always be on the second line or second space above or below the position of the given note.

EXAMPLE.   If given note is  , a perfect fifth above is

If given note is , a perfect fifth below is

EXERCISE 7. Write the second note a perfect fifth above the given note.

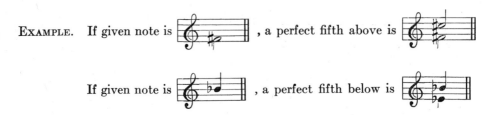

EXERCISE 8. Write the second note a perfect fifth below the given note.

EXERCISE 9. Play a perfect fifth placing the second note above the given note.

EXERCISE 10. Play a perfect fifth placing the second note below the given note.

The tempered perfect fourth contains five tempered half-tones, and it is slightly larger than the just perfect fourth. This is understandable, since the just perfect fifth and the just perfect fourth added together equal an octave.

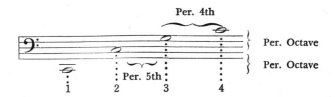

Now, the above same tones, played in tempered tuning, reveal that the perfect octaves 1 and 2, and 2 and 4 are in tune, but the perfect fifth, 2 and 3, is slightly smaller. This would obviously make 3 and 4, the perfect fourth (4/3), slightly larger because the interval 2 and 4, which is an octave, is in tune. Also, it is to be observed that if the lower note of a perfect fifth is placed an octave higher, the resulting interval will be a perfect fourth; likewise, if the upper note of the perfect fifth is placed an octave lower, the resulting interval will also be a perfect fourth.

To form an *inverted interval* of any given interval, change the relative position of the two notes, either by placing the lower note an octave higher or the upper note an octave lower.

EXERCISE 11. Form the perfect fourth by placing the lower note of the perfect fifth an octave higher.

EXERCISE 12. Form the perfect fourth by placing the upper note of the perfect fifth an octave lower.

From the preceding exercises you have learned that the component tones of the perfect fourth have the same accidental, with the exception of the interval of the fourth built on f, which has the spelling f to b♭ or f♯ to b.

EXERCISE 13. Write the second note a perfect fourth above the given note.

EXERCISE 14. Write the second note a perfect fourth below the given note.

EXERCISE 15. Play a perfect fourth placing the second note above the given note.

EXERCISE 16. Play a perfect fourth placing the second note below the given note.

The tempered major third contains four half-tones, and it is slightly larger than the just major third. A third may be obtained by counting three letters upwards or downwards. For example:

the third above d is as follows:

    f   3
      e 2
    d 1

the third below b is as follows:

    b   3
      a 2
    g 1

In equal temperament tuning, not all thirds found in the musical alphabet are major thirds. The major thirds which are found are as follows: c to e; f to a; g to b. The component tones of these major thirds will always have the same accidentals, namely, c♭ to e♭; c♯ to e♯; g♭ to b♭; etc.; the following thirds are found containing three half-tones: d to f; e to g; a to c; b to d. The component tones of these intervals will always have the accidental arrangement from the lower tone to the higher tone in the following order:

> Upper Tone: ♭ (♮)* ♯ ✕
> Lower Tone: ♭♭ ♭ (♮)* ♯

EXERCISE 17. Give the spelling of the tone a major third above the following tones: e; g♭; a♭; c♯; f♭; b; d♯; e♭.

Give the spelling of the tone a major third below the following tones: d; a♭; b♭; g; c♭; f✕; g♯; a♯.

* The natural sign is not written unless the signature makes it necessary.

To locate the interval of the third on the staff, the second note will always be on the first line or first space above or below the position of the given note.

EXAMPLE.   If given note is , a major third above is

If given note is , a major third below is

EXERCISE 18. Write the second note a major third above the given note.

EXERCISE 19. Write the second note a major third below the given note.

EXERCISE 20. Play a major third, placing the second note above the given note.

EXERCISE 21. Play a major third, placing the second note below the given note.

The tempered minor third contains three half-tones, and it is slightly smaller than the just minor third.   In equal temperament tuning, the minor thirds found in the musical alphabet are as follows: a to c; b to d; d to f; e to g.   The component tones of these minor thirds will always have the same accidentals, namely, d to f; d♯ to f♯; b♭ to d♭; etc.   The following thirds contain four half-tones; c to e; f to a; g to b.   The component tones of these intervals, when their spellings are to form a minor third, will have the accidental arrangement from the lower tone to the higher tone in the following order:

Upper Tone: ♭♭ ♭ ♮
Lower Tone: ♭ ♮ ♯

EXERCISE 22. Give the spelling of the tone a minor third above the following tones: e; b; db; f; c♯; ab; g; f♯.

Give the spelling of the tone a minor third below the following tones: ab; f♯; b; g♯; d; eb; a; c.

EXERCISE 23. Write the second note a minor third above the given note.

EXERCISE 24. Write the second note a minor third below the given note.

EXERCISE 25. Play a minor third, placing the second note above the given note.

EXERCISE 26. Play a minor third, placing the second note below the given note.

$\mathcal{C}$hapter 14

The Chord

The composers and theorists of the 18th and 19th centuries are indebted to Jean Philippe Rameau (1683–1764) for the theory of harmony generally accepted during this period. In 1722 he published the *Traité de l'harmonie réduit à ses principes naturels*, which challenged the prevailing pedagogical procedures, as well as the very foundations upon which occidental music was built. This epochal treatise of 1722 and subsequent studies were concerned with revealing that the music of his time arose from the arithmetical, geometric, and harmonic divisions of the vibrating string. Although Rameau, in describing his views, established principles which survived the test of time, he made miscalculations, as does every great innovator.

Harmony in its broadest meaning is the aural effect which is brought about by the union of musical tones. Before Rameau's treatises the musician calculated the consonant and dissonant elements in a sonority from the lowest tone of that sonority.

In the following example, the sonorities at (*a*), (*b*), and (*c*) were calculated and identified as consonant sonorities from their respective bass tones.

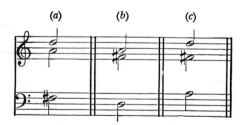

It is to be observed that each sonority in the example is composed of d, f-sharp, and a; but in each case the tones are in a different arrangement.

It is with this point of view concerning analysis of a sonority that Rameau proposed his revolutionary theory. He believed that the sonorities at (*a*), (*b*), and

(c) in the previous example should be identified as the same sound.   The basic sonority was (b), and the sonorities at (a) and (c) were other possible forms.

In proving his theory Rameau used a series of monochords.*   Continuing his explanation of the preceding discussion, let us consider that eight strings are tuned in unison at the pitch of Great D, as illustrated.   The first is permitted to vibrate as a whole, and the others vibrate in 2, 3, 4, 5, and 6 parts respectively.   Their frequencies are represented on the staff.

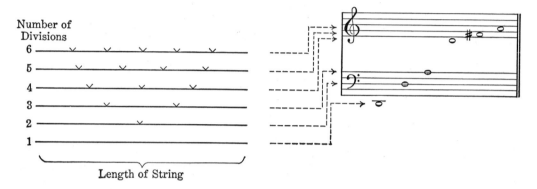

At the point where the strings are divided into 4, 5, and 6 segments, we obtain the d, f-sharp, and a, which was the sonority found in the example on page 67.

Applied to this experiment, Rameau's theory states that Great D is the fundamental tone of this sonority and that all other possible d's, f-sharps, and a's are derived from the Great D, since the small d, small a, d^1, f-sharp^1, and a^1 were produced by dividing the Great D into 2, 3, 4, 5, and 6 segments respectively.

In addition, Rameau points out that the musician's musical thought processes will react to this same sonority in such a way as to select d as the most important tone in the sonorities of the example on page 67.   The musical intellect collects the tones and tends to arrange them in a series of thirds within an octave.   This arrangement usually takes place in the musical thought processes in a pitch area corresponding to the auditor's vocal range.†

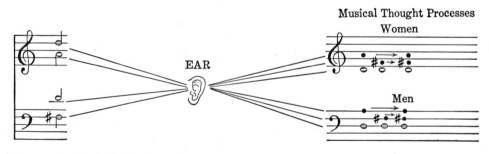

* A monochord is a scientific instrument which is composed of a sound-box over which is stretched a single string.   By means of a movable bridge or a group of movable bridges the string may be divided at any point.

† The concept that what takes place in one octave is transferable to lower or higher octaves without changing the musical meaning is a musical axiom.

Training of the musical intellect enables the musician to isolate any one of the tones of the sonority played and to discuss its relation to the whole sonority.

Sonorities which are analyzed by musical thought processes as tonal structures built in thirds are called *chords*.* Triads are chords composed of three tones which are arranged a third apart, and seventh chords are composed of four tones which are arranged a third apart.

According to Rameau's theories, the following conclusions regarding the music of the 18th and 19th centuries may be drawn:

1. The chord is the essential basis for the construction of the music.
2. The tones of a chord may be rearranged without having the chord lose its fundamental and, accordingly, its identity. This concept is the *theory of inversion*. Recognition of the fundamental of a chord is not destroyed when chord members are rearranged so that the fundamental tone does not appear in the bass.

* Since 1900 composers have introduced chords built in other intervals. These chords, however, do not fit into the styles of the 18th and 19th century composition.

Chapter 15

The Major Triad

The most frequent chord encountered in the music of the 18th and 19th centuries is the major triad. Historically, it came into being through the union of the perfect fifth and major third erected upon the same tone.

In this example, the lowest tone is the *root* or *fundamental*. The tone a major third above the root is the *third*. The tone a perfect fifth above the root is the *fifth*. The major triad built on any tone is identified by the name of that note. For instance, the triad illustrated is called the f-major triad. The best way to analyze aurally the major triad is to break it up into intervals related to the root, instead of trying to hear it as composed of thirds built one upon the other. The major triad suggests a major third in combination with a perfect fifth built upon the same bass tone.

SPELLING THE MAJOR TRIAD

The aural effect of the major triad suggests a rapid and accurate method for spelling a major triad on any of the twelve tones in the octave. To spell any major triad on a given root, spell the tone a major third above the root, spell the tone a perfect fifth above the root, and recite the triad, spelling in the order of the root, third, and fifth. For example, spell the a-major triad. A major third above a is c-sharp; a perfect fifth above a is e; the a-major triad spelling is a-c♯-e.

EXERCISE 1. Be able to spell any major triad.
EXERCISE 2. Place the major triad on the staff, considering each given tone as the root.

EXERCISE 3. Play the major triad, considering each given tone as the root.

Right hand

Left hand

PLAYING THE MAJOR TRIAD IN FOUR VOICES

In elementary theory, traditional musical instruction favors the study of chords in four voices, namely, soprano, alto, tenor, and bass. The ranges of the voices are as follows:

The whole notes and the range between represent the highest frequency. The dark notes on either side of the whole notes vary in size. The largest is more frequent than the smallest.

Since a triad contains three tones, it will be necessary to double one of these tones if the triad is played or written in four voices. This doubling may be at the unison or at a distance of one, two, or three octaves. When a major triad is played with the root in the bass, it is customary to double the root.

The spacing of the tones which make up the triad is of real importance. In the following examples, notice the freedom given the bass in its interval relationship to the tenor, alto, and soprano.

A chord in which the interval between tenor and soprano is an octave or less is in *close structure*.

Close Structure

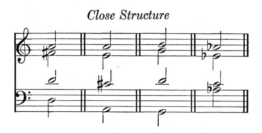

A chord in which the interval between the tenor and soprano is greater than an octave is in *open structure*.

Open Structure

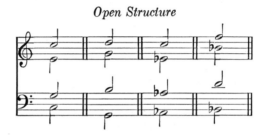

The term *position* refers to whichever chord member is found in the soprano. A major triad is in the *position of the octave* when the root is in the soprano. A major triad is in the *position of the third* when the third is in the soprano. A major triad is in the *position of the fifth* when the fifth is in the soprano.

EXERCISE 4. Play any major triad in the position of the octave, third, or fifth.
            Instructions: Cover the given chord with the left hand so that the fifth finger
                          rests on the root. The right hand then arranges the chord
                          spelling so that the root, third, or fifth is in the soprano.
           Example: Play the d-major triad in the position of the third.

The *first inversion* of a triad has the third in the bass. Terminology for obtaining a desired soprano in the first inversion of a major triad is as follows:

(*a*) The first inversion of the a-major triad in the position of the octave.

(*b*) The first inversion of the d-flat major triad in the position of the third.

(*c*) The first inversion of the e-flat major triad in the position of the fifth.

In the chords at (*a*), (*b*), and (*c*), observe that the tone in the soprano is doubled in one of the lower voices. For the present, the soprano will be doubled in the first inversion of a major triad.

EXERCISE 5. Play the first inversion of any major triad in the position of either the octave, third, or fifth.

Example: Play the first inversion of the e-flat major triad in the position of the fifth.

The *second inversion* of a triad has the fifth in the bass. Terminology for obtaining a desired soprano tone in the second inversion of a major triad is as follows:

(*a*) The second inversion of the a-flat major triad in the position of the octave.

(*b*) The second inversion of the b-major triad in the position of the third.

(*c*) The second inversion of the d-major triad in the position of the fifth.

In the chords at (*a*), (*b*), and (*c*), observe that the tone in the bass is doubled in one of the upper voices. The bass tone will be doubled in the second inversion of a major triad.

EXERCISE 6. Play the second inversion of any major triad in the position of either the octave, third, or fifth.

Example: Play the second inversion of the g-major triad in the position of the octave.

THE APPLICATION OF THE THEORY OF INVERSION*

EXERCISE 7. Be able to recognize the root of a major triad.

Example: A series of major triads will be played. Listen to the triad and sing the root, using a neutral syllable.

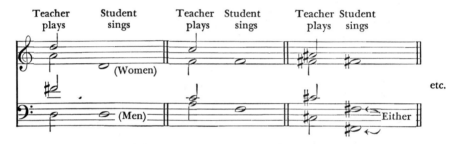

As soon as the root of a major triad is accurately located, the next step in listening to the major triad is to recognize the root, third, or fifth in the soprano. A major triad is played. (1) Using a neutral syllable, sing the root; (2) sing the soprano; (3) listen to the relationship between the root and the soprano tone. The root, third, or fifth in the soprano is identified by the following analysis:

a. If the soprano possesses a feeling of rest, it is the *root*.

b. If the soprano descends directly by leap to the root and no chord tone is between, it is the *third*.

c. If the soprano tone descends through the third to the root, it is the *fifth*.

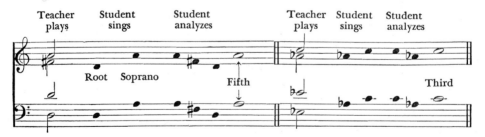

* See conclusion (2), page 69.

Carry on this procedure until the chord member is easily identified in the soprano. The following chords briefly illustrate the way in which the drill is to be continued:

EXERCISE 8. Identify the root, third, or fifth in the soprano of a major triad.
> Example: A series of major triads will be played. Listen to the soprano and determine whether it is the root, third, or fifth.

> This exercise may be practised with the student giving first oral and then written response. When writing, use
>> 1 for the root
>> 3 for the third
>> 5 for the fifth
> The written answer for the above example would appear as follows:
>> 1 5 5 3 1
>> 5 3 3 1 5

Before identifying the chord members in the bass, be sure that the student can locate and sing on a neutral syllable the bass tone of a major triad. For this drill use a series of major triads, varying the chord member in the bass.

EXERCISE 9. Identify the root, third, or fifth in the bass.
> Example: A series of major triads will be played. Listen to the bass and determine whether it is the root, third, or fifth.

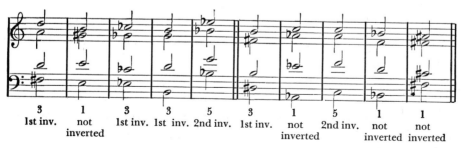

Using other chords, this exercise at first should be given oral response as follows:

1 for the root		not inverted for the root
3 for the third	or	first inversion for the third
5 for the fifth		second inversion for the fifth

As a written response, the above exercise is to appear as follows:

3 1 3 3 5

3 1 5 1 1

Or as follows: 1st inv.—not inverted—1st inv.—1st inv.   —2nd inv.

1st inv.—not inverted—2nd inv.—not inverted—not inverted

EXERCISE 10. Locating and determining which chord member is in the soprano and bass.

Example: Major triads will be played in any of the nine possible arrangements. First, sing, using a neutral syllable, the root and then the soprano, secondly the root and then the bass, finally sing the bass and the soprano with the correct chord member numbers.

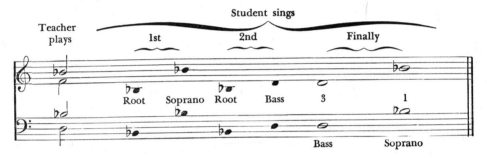

EXERCISE 11. Identify the root, third, or fifth in the soprano and bass of a major triad.

Example: Major triads will be played in any of the nine possible arrangements. Listen to the bass and soprano and determine their respective chord members.

Using other chords, this exercise should be given at first oral response, later written response. As a written response, the above exercise is to appear as follows:

Soprano 3 1 3 5 1   1 5 1 1 3

Bass   1 5 3 3 5   3 5 1 1 3

As soon as the chord member drill is achieved, continue the previous exercise describing the triad using terminology. In terminology the first three chords of the above example are as follows:

1. A major triad in the position of the third.

2. The second inversion of a major triad in the position of the octave.

3. The first inversion of a major triad in the position of the third.

Having learned to spell, play, and recognize chord members in the bass and soprano, the next step will be to identify a major triad by name, when the pitch name of the soprano tone of the triad which is to be played, is given. For example,

if  is given and the following chord is played 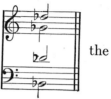 the d flat

is heard as the fifth which will identify the chord as g♭ b♭ d♭. Since the third is heard in the bass, the complete chord is identified as the first inversion of the g-flat major triad in the position of the third. The triad is to be written on staff paper in the same manner as it is played. (Playing all nine possible arrangements of the soprano and bass has been learned.)

EXERCISE 12. Writing the major triad in four voices on staff paper from dictation when the soprano tone is given.
　　　　Example: The instructor names "d" in the soprano and plays the second inversion of the b-flat major triad in the position of the third. The student's solution appears as follows:

Performing this exercise for a series of chords, on the blackboard copy the soprano tones which are to be used in the following manner:

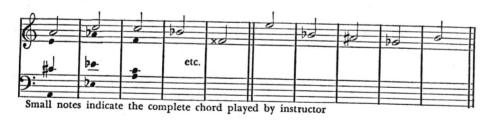

Small notes indicate the complete chord played by instructor

EXERCISE 13. Describing a chord from dictation when the soprano tone is known.
　　　　Example: The instructor names c-sharp as the soprano tone.

Instructor plays: Student recites or writes: The first inversion of the f-sharp major triad in the position of the fifth

THE TONAL ELEMENTS

PART-WRITING THE MAJOR TRIAD

Thus far the major triad has been played in close structure and placed on the staff from dictation in close structure. However, triads are used in both close and open structure. A triad which has its fundamental in the bass may be converted from close structure to open structure by inverting the alto and tenor tones.

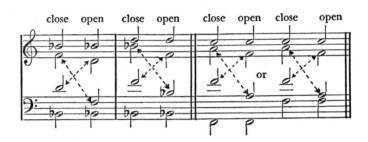

EXERCISE 14. Convert the close structure of a major triad into open structure.*
    Note: each chord must have two roots, a third, and a fifth. Observe the pitch range of the alto and tenor.

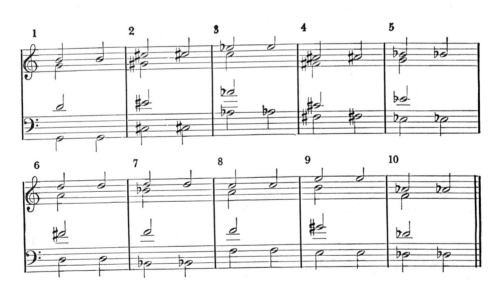

When a triad is repeated with a new position in the soprano, move the three upper voices in similar motion, retaining the close or open structure of the first chord.

---

  * Beginning with Exercise 14 and continuing through this chapter, the exercises should not be solved in the text. These exercises are to be used as additional keyboard drills. The bass and tenor should now be played by the left hand.

Retaining Close Structure

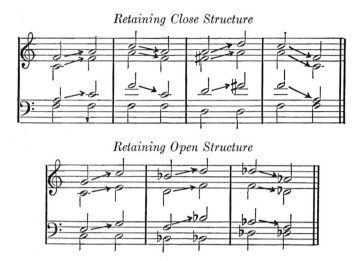

Retaining Open Structure

Exercise 15. Retain the structure of the first chord in the second chord.

When a triad is repeated with a new position in the soprano, change from open to close structure or the reverse is achieved by retaining one of the inner voices on the same pitch while the other inner voice will exchange tones with the soprano, either at the octave or at the unison.

Example:

EXERCISE 16. Change the structure of the second chord.

The best tone to double in the first inversion of a major triad is the soprano, which may be either the root or fifth. The first inversion of a major triad in the position of the third (considered as having either a doubled soprano or doubled bass) is used less in four-voice composition, but it is by no means infrequent. When a major triad is followed by its first inversion or the reverse, the upper voices move to the voices of the second chord according to the following principles:

1. As the root moves to the third in the bass, reverse this movement in an upper voice, and the other voices remain stationary.
2. One or two upper voices move in similar motion to the bass; the other voice or voices, as the case might be, remain stationary.
3. One or two upper voices move in contrary motion to the bass; the other voice or voices remain stationary.
4. The third and root in one voice interchange with the bass; the remaining voices interchange their fifth and root.

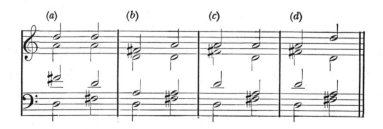

When a major triad in the position of the third is followed by the first inversion of the same triad in the position of the third, the three upper voices remain stationary. This harmonic situation is found infrequently in four-voice writing.

EXERCISE 17. A major triad is followed by its first inversion.   Add the alto and tenor.

EXERCISE 18. A major triad in first inversion is followed by the same triad with root in the
bass.   Add the alto and tenor.

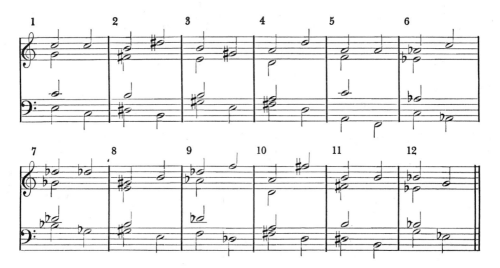

Chapter 16

Intervals and the Major Triad

In Rameau's *Traité de l'harmonie* the explanation of the origin of the consonant intervals is found in the harmonic division of the vibrating strings. If c^1 and f^1 are produced, the ratio of their frequencies, based on $a^1 = 440$ dv., is 264:352. Reducing this ratio to small numbers, we obtain 3:4. Locating c^1 and f^1 in a harmonic series, we find that the fundamental of the series is F. In like manner, if a^1 (440 dv) and c^2 (528 dv) are produced, the ratio of their frequencies, reduced to small numbers, is 5:6. The fundamental of the series still remains F.

Rameau went one step further, arguing that these intervals imply a third tone, the resulting sound being a chord. For example, any intervallic combinations of the above f's, a's, and c's will imply the f-major triad. This point of view is in direct agreement with the manner in which the composers wrote their music at his time and through the 19th century. Tones in a musical composition which can be identified as chord members are called *essential tones*.

Let us observe just how Rameau's theory, that an *interval implies a chord*, works out in actual musical composition.

Example:*

Der Tag, der ist so freudenreich   J. Pachelbel

Implied harmony

* *Note:* The tones marked x are tones which do not belong to the harmony. They are *unessential tones* and are called *non-harmonic tones.*

82

In the next example, note how an interval formed by a succession of tones in a melody implies a chord.

Op. 12, No. 3 (Rondo)   L. von Beethoven

Implied harmony

These examples tend to prove the correctness of Rameau's theory. Since the music of the 18th and 19th centuries uses intervals which imply chords, it is logical to study intervals in relation to chords.

EXERCISE 1. Playing intervallic relationships.
  The instructor names a triad to which the student is to play combinations of the root, third, or fifth. The student covers the triad with the left hand and plays the desired intervallic relationship in the right hand.
  Example: Play 3 up to 5 in the d-major triad.

EXERCISE 2. Sing any intervallic relationship from a given pitch based on a major triad.
  The instructor plays any pitch and directs the student to use it as root, third, or fifth and to sing any relationship of root, third, or fifth above or below.
  Example: Consider the given pitch as 5. Sing 5 down to 1.

EXERCISE 3. Recognize the intervallic relationship based on a major triad.
  The instructor, at the piano, plays an interval ascending or descending, based on a major triad. Identify the implied chord members.
  Example:

Instructor plays: Student recites: 3 up to 5
                                   or
                           writes: 3 u 5
                           (Use "d" for down)

A *melodic interval* is one in which the two tones follow each other.   In an *harmonic interval* the two tones are sounded simultaneously.   Practise Exercise 3, playing the interval harmonically.   The lowest tone is identified first.

Example:

Instructor plays: Student recites: 5–1
                                  or
                        writes: 1
                                  5

The relationship between the chord members and the name of the interval is as follows:

Chord Members*	Name of Interval	Chord Members	Name of Interval
1 u 1		1 u 3	Major Third
3 u 3		3 d 1	
5 u 5			
	· Perfect Octave	3 u 5	Minor Third
1 d 1		5 d 3	
3 d 3			
5 d 5		5 u 3	Major Sixth
		3 d 5	
1 u 5	Perfect Fifth		
5 d 1		3 u 1	Minor Sixth
		1 d 3	
5 u 1	Perfect Fourth		
1 d 5			

EXERCISE 4. Recognizing the chord members and naming the interval.   The instructor plays the various intervals, either melodically or harmonically.   The student determines the chord members and names the interval.

Example:

Instructor plays:

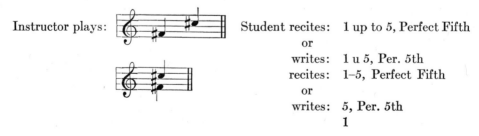

Student recites: 1 up to 5, Perfect Fifth
                          or
               writes: 1 u 5, Per. 5th
               recites: 1–5, Perfect Fifth
                          or
               writes: 5, Per. 5th
                         1

* u = up; d = down.

EXERCISE 5. The interval placed on the staff from dictation. The instructor names the first note if the interval is to be played melodically, or the lowest note if the interval is to be played harmonically. This note is placed on the staff. After the interval is heard, the student determines the chord members and writes the chord on the bass clef; then writes the second note. The name of the interval is placed directly below the written interval.

Example: The instructor names d-flat.*

Instructor plays: Student responds:

Maj. 6th

EXERCISE 6. Intervals dictated melodically or harmonically.* Instructor follows the same procedure as in Exercise 5. The student writes only the interval on the staff and its name.

THE INVERSION OF THE INTERVAL

Just as the triad may be inverted without affecting its root, in like manner, the interval may be inverted without affecting the harmonic background.

Example:

M 3rd   m 6th   Per. 4th   Per. 5th

Table of Inversion of Interval

Given interval	Interval inverted
Unison	Perfect Octave
Perfect Octave	Perfect Unison
Perfect Fifth	Perfect Fourth
Perfect Fourth	Perfect Fifth
Major Third	Minor Sixth
Minor Third	Major Sixth
Major Sixth	Minor Third
Minor Sixth	Major Third

From the above table the following deductions can be made:

1. Perfect intervals when inverted remain perfect.
2. Major intervals when inverted become minor.
3. Minor intervals when inverted become major.

* For variety, the name of the upper tone in the harmonic interval may sometimes be given.

EXERCISE 7. Place on staff paper, using the treble clef, the inversion and name of interval for the following harmonic intervals:

1. major third built on d-flat
2. perfect fifth built on f-sharp
3. perfect octave built on e
4. minor sixth built on f-double sharp
5. perfect fourth built on e-flat
6. major sixth built on d-sharp
7. minor sixth built on d-sharp
8. perfect fifth built on c-sharp
9. unison built on g
10. minor third built on e-flat

Chapter 17

The Minor Triad

The next frequent chord encountered in the music of the 18th and 19th centuries is the minor triad. Like the major triad, the minor triad can be regarded as a union of the perfect fifth and third erected upon the same tone.

Per. 5th   m.3rd

From an aural point of view the minor triad suggests a minor third in combination with a perfect fifth derived from the same root.

SPELLING THE MINOR TRIAD

To spell any minor triad on a given root, spell the tone a minor third above the root, spell the tone a perfect fifth above the root, and recite the triad in the order of the root, third, and fifth. For example, spell the f-sharp minor triad. A minor third above f-sharp is a; a perfect fifth above f-sharp is c-sharp; the f-sharp minor triad is f♯ a c♯.

EXERCISE 1. Be able to spell orally any minor triad when the spelling of the root is specified
EXERCISE 2. Place the minor triad on the staff considering each given note as the root.

87

EXERCISE 3. Play the minor triad considering each given note as the root.

PLAYING THE MINOR TRIAD IN FOUR VOICES

As in the major triad, double the root when playing the minor triad in the position of the octave, third, or fifth.

EXERCISE 4. Play any minor triad in the position of the octave, third, or fifth.
   Example: Play the b-minor triad in the position of the octave.

When playing the first inversion of a minor triad, double the soprano tone.

EXERCISE 5. Play the first inversion of any minor triad in the position of the octave, third, or fifth.
   Example: Play the first inversion of the c-minor triad in the position of the third.

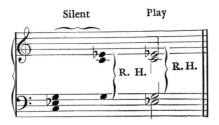

When playing the second inversion of a minor triad, double the bass tone.

EXERCISE 6. Play the second inversion of a minor triad in the position of the octave, third, or fifth.

Example: Play the second inversion of the b-flat minor triad in the position of the octave.

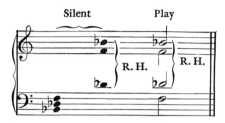

THE APPLICATION OF THE THEORY OF INVERSION

EXERCISE 7. Be able to recognize the root of a minor triad.

Example: A series of minor triads will be played. Listen to the triad and then sing the root, using a neutral syllable.

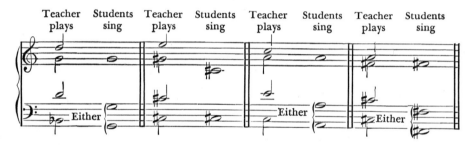

The procedure established in Exercises 8, 9, and 10 of Chapter 15 is to be followed in the next three exercises.

EXERCISE 8. Identify the root, third, or fifth in the soprano of a minor triad.
EXERCISE 9. Identify the root, third, or fifth in the bass of a minor triad.
EXERCISE 10. Identify the root, third, or fifth in the soprano and the bass of a minor triad.
EXERCISE 11. Identify a major triad or a minor triad.

Example: A phrase of music will be played. As the phrase is repeated identify orally or in writing the type of each triad. When writing, use M for a major triad; m for a minor triad.

EXERCISE 12. Identify a major triad and a minor triad; in addition, give the soprano and bass of each triad.

Example: A phrase of music will be played which contains major and minor triads. As the phrase is repeated, identify the type triad and its soprano and bass.

The oral or written response is in terminology. The answer for the first three triads in the example above is as follows:

1. minor triad in the position of the third.
2. first inversion of a major triad in the position of the octave.
3. first inversion of a major triad in the position of the octave.

EXERCISE 13. Writing the minor triad in four voices on the staff from dictation when the soprano is given.

Example: The instructor names c-sharp in the soprano and plays the first inversion of the f-sharp minor triad in the position of the fifth. The student's solution appears as follows:

For a series of chords, the student is given the soprano tones as follows:

EXERCISE 14. Describing a minor triad from dictation when the soprano tone is known.

Example: The instructor names b-flat as the soprano tone.

Instructor plays: Student recites or writes: e-flat minor triad in the position of the fifth

EXERCISE 15. Writing the major and minor triads in four voices on the staff from dictation when the soprano tone is given.   Use the same procedure as in Exercise 13.

EXERCISE 16. Describing major and minor triads when the soprano tone is known.   Use the same procedure as in Exercise 14.

PART-WRITING THE MINOR TRIAD

The part-writing procedures for the minor triad and the major triad are the same.   In four voices a minor triad with its root in the bass has two roots, a third and a fifth.   Under normal conditions the interval between the consecutive voices, soprano and alto or alto and tenor, is never greater than an octave.

EXERCISE 17. In each example change the structure in the second chord.*

EXERCISE 18. Retain the structure of the first chord in the second chord.

* Exercises 17 through 21 are to be used for part-writing as well as keyboard drills.   The student is not to fill in the voices in the text.   When solving these exercises at the keyboard, the tenor and bass voices are to be played with the left hand; the soprano and alto are to be played with the right hand.

EXERCISE 19. Change the structure of the second chord.

EXERCISE 20. A minor triad is followed by its first inversion. Add the alto and tenor.

EXERCISE 21. A minor triad in first inversion is followed by the same triad with the root in the bass. Add the alto and tenor.

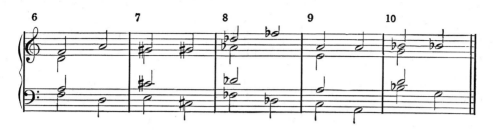

Chapter 18

Intervals and the Minor Triad

The intervals which imply a minor triad are the same as those which imply a major triad. The perfect intervals are in the same position for both the major and minor triads; for example, the perfect fifth e-b implies either the E-major triad or the e-minor triad. This, however, is not true of the major and minor intervals; for instance, the major third e-g♯ implies either root and third of the E-major triad or third and fifth of the c-sharp minor triad.

For this reason, it is imperative that the student of music train himself to recognize with equal facility the chordal implications possible for each interval.

EXERCISE 1. Playing intervallic relationships.
    The instructor names a triad to which the student is to play combinations of the root, third, or fifth. The student covers the triad with the left hand and plays the desired intervallic relationship in the right hand.
    Example: Play 3 up to 1 in the c-minor triad.

EXERCISE 2. Sing any intervallic relationship from a given pitch based on a minor triad.
    The instructor plays any pitch and directs the student to use it as root, third, or fifth and to sing any relationship of root, third, or fifth above or below.
    Example: Consider the given pitch as 5. Sing 5 down to 3.

EXERCISE 3. Recognize the intervallic relationship based on a minor triad.
The instructor, at the piano, plays an interval ascending or descending, based on a minor triad. Identify the implied chord members.
Example:

Instructor plays: Student recites: 5 up to 3
                                                 or
                                    writes: 5 u 3

This exercise should also be drilled, using harmonic intervals.
Example:

Instructor plays: Student recites: 5–3
                                        or
                                  writes: 3
                                                           5

In a minor triad the relationship between the chord members and the name of the interval is as follows:

Chord Members	Name of Interval	Chord Members	Name of Interval
1 u 1 3 u 3 5 u 5 1 d 1 3 d 3 5 d 5	Perfect Octave	1 u 3 3 d 1	Minor Third
		3 u 5 5 d 3	Major Third
1 u 5 5 d 1	Perfect Fifth	3 u 1 1 d 3	Major Sixth
5 u 1 1 d 5	Perfect Fourth	5 u 3 3 d 5	Minor Sixth

EXERCISE 4. Recognizing the chord members and naming the interval. The instructor plays the various intervals, either melodically or harmonically. The student determines the chord members and names the interval.
Example:

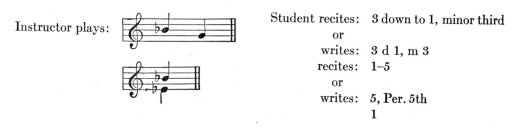

Instructor plays: Student recites: 3 down to 1, minor third
                                       or
                                writes: 3 d 1, m 3
                                recites: 1–5
                                       or
                                writes: 5, Per. 5th
                                                           1

EXERCISE 5. The interval placed on the staff from dictation.
            Example: The instructor names c-sharp.

Instructor plays: Student responds:

EXERCISE 6. Intervals dictated melodically or harmonically.*
            The instructor follows the same procedure as in Exercise 5. The student
            writes only the interval on the staff and gives its name.

* When dictating the harmonic interval, give the name of either the lower or upper tone.

Chapter 19
The Concept of Tonality

Thus far in our pursuit of the fundamental principles of occidental 18th and 19th century music, the elements of time, rhythm, intervals, and chords have been presented. We have not, however, considered the manner in which tones are related in a given period time. The fact that a piece of music must begin and end is probably the most predominant concept which has guided the composer through the ages. The manifestation of this idea is musical form. As one listens to a composition, important and less important beginnings and important and less important endings reveal themselves during the progress of the music. This principle is always perceptible.

This point of view leads us to adopt the theory that in every period of music there is law and order in the handling of sounds which make up the composition. It has always been the author's contention that a broader interpretation ought to be applied to the term *tonality*. In its more liberal application *tonality* consists of the perception of a succession of musical sounds in such a manner as to create and maintain a mental background of continuity, in which the separate events, remaining clear and distinct, become the logical elements of a united whole. Tonality is, then, the guiding force that made possible the Gregorian Chant and the music of such great masters as Dunstable, Dufay, Palestrina, Lassus, Monteverde, Beethoven, Debussy, and many others. If these men had not carefully maintained in their music the idea of a "background of continuity, in which the separate events, remaining clear and distinct, become the logical elements of a united whole," their music could not have survived.

The art of music would have become extinct if it had not been for the unceasing desire on the part of the composers of the past to seek new ways to express their musical thoughts. Many devoted considerable effort to determining how they put their music together. It is, therefore, important for us to realize that Philippe Rameau's research into the tonality of his own music and that of his contemporaries contributes much to our understanding of the significance of the key center.

97

THE MAJOR AND MINOR KEYS

It was Rameau's belief that major and minor keys were established by chord progression. Having satisfied himself that his theory of inversion was sound, his first step was to write, on a third staff placed below each line of the score, the root of every chord. The succession of roots on the accompanying staff below each line of a composition is called the *fundamental bass* by Rameau. His next step in the analysis was to study the interval between consecutive fundamental bass notes. The fundamental bass to three chorales harmonized by three of Rameau's contemporaries is as follows:

Was Gott thut, das ist wohlgethan   J. S. Bach

Fundamental bass

Herzliebster Jesu, was hast du verbrochen C. H. Graun

Fundamental bass

Ach Gott und Herr G. Handel

Fundamental bass

Considering the interval of the fourth as the inversion of the fifth, the intervals appear in the fundamental bass of the above examples in this frequency:

Composer	Prime*	Fifth	Third	Second	Total
J. S. Bach	6	26	4	2	38
C. H. Graun	4	19	6	10	39
G. F. Handel	3	22	0	6	31
Total	13	67	10	18	108

Continuing this study and using compositions by Bach, Graun, Handel, and Telemann it appears that in over five thousand successive chord movements the prime, fifth, second, and third had the following usage:†

		Prime	Fifth	Second	Third
J. S. Bach	(1685–1750)	16%	52%	21%	11%
G. F. Handel	(1685–1759)	6	59	29	6
C. H. Graun	(c. 1703–1759)	6	64	18	12
G. P. Telemann	(1681–1767)	12	55	23	10
Average percentage		10	57.5	22.75	9.75

Although Rameau did not consider the prime, the above table is in agreement with his observation, which is that "chords progress most often with their roots a fifth apart; next often, with their roots a second apart; and least often, with their roots a third apart."

In the *Traité* he stresses the fact that the best root movement is down a fifth. The author investigated this, and he presents the following deductions.‡

* Rameau does not mention in his *Traité de l'harmonie* the fact that chords may be repeated. The author, however, maintains that this is likewise an important factor in the study of root movement. Although Rameau occasionally refers to the relation of harmonic movement and rhythm, there is practically no development of this concept in any of his treatises.

† These composers were selected because they were composing during the period in which Rameau was writing his treatises on the music of his time. The type of music selected, from the above composers, includes arias, choral compositions, instrumental, etc., but not recitatives.

For those interested in research into a style, see Allen I. McHose, *Musical Research in the Definition of Bach's Contrapuntal Harmonic Style.* Pittsburgh: Volume of Proceedings for 1948 of the Music Teachers National Association, pp. 126 through 150.

‡ The information in this table plays an important rôle in the concept of the classification of root movement, Chapter 22.

The Chord Progression	Roots Ascending	Roots Descending
roots a fifth apart	less frequent	frequent
roots a second apart	frequent	infrequent
roots a third apart	infrequent	frequent

Rameau, quite convinced that root movement a fifth apart was the basis of the music of his time, continued to investigate its characteristics. Through this research he observed that the most frequent roots which appeared in the course of a musical composition could be arranged in a series of two fifths.*

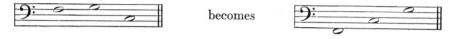

becomes

Furthermore, he found that the root which was in the center of such a fifth arrangement became the root of the last chord of the composition.

Rameau then suggests erecting a major triad on each root in the example above and writing a composition using these three chords. He says that one will perceive that the c-major triad becomes the harmony upon which the composition must close.

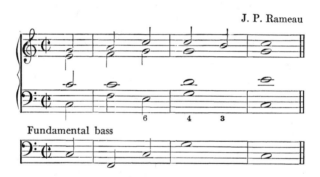

J. P. Rameau

Fundamental bass

Again this concept is illustrated by a portion of a Bach Chorale in which only the c-major, g-major, and d-major triads are utilized.

Lobt Gott, ihr Christen allgugleich

J. S. Bach

1st phrase

Fundamental bass

* The author found this to be true but obtained a lower frequency for the note f, since he does not recognize Rameau's analysis of the first inversion of the supertonic seventh chord as a subdominant triad with an added sixth.

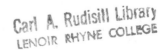

From this discussion, our definition of a major key which is in accord with that of Rameau is as follows: A *Major Key* results from the arrangement of three major triads whose roots are consecutively systematized in perfect fifths.   The center triad identifies the key.*   For example, the key of e-flat is established as follows:

Subdominant Tonic   Dominant

Rameau called the triad which determines the key, the *tonic triad*.   The triad which has its root a fifth above the root of the tonic triad is the *dominant triad*. The triad which has its root a fifth below the root of the tonic triad is the *subdominant triad*.

Before presenting the theory of the major scale,† one should ponder over Sir Hubert Parry's oft-quoted opinion.‡   He says,

It is advisable to guard at the outset against the familiar misconception that scales are made first and music afterwards.   Scales are made in the process of endeavoring to make music, and continue to be altered and modified, generation after generation, even till the art has arrived at a high degree of maturity.   The scale of modern music, which European peoples use, only arrived at its present condition in the last [i.e., the 18th] century, after having been under a gradual process of modification from an accepted nucleus for nearly a thousand years.

Even today there remain presentations of elementary theory which teach that the major and minor keys are established by the use of the major and minor scales. Some of these methods grossly misrepresent the entire concept of key feeling by making a minor key subservient to a major key.   With this in mind, the author wishes to emphasize the theories of Rameau and subsequent theoretical scholars who stress the fact that the music of the 18th and 19th century is based on the characteristics of the fundamental bass progressions and that major and minor scales result from the type of chords erected on these fundamental bass tones.

A careful examination of the example below reveals that the sum of all the different tones found in the arrangement of the tonic, dominant, and subdominant chords, is seven.   If these seven tones beginning on e-flat are placed in alphabetical order, the result is the e-flat major scale.   The major scale can, therefore, be derived from the consistent use of a major tonic triad, major dominant triad, and major subdominant triad.   The scale derived in this way is called the *diatonic major scale*.§

* See Appendix V for the physicist's explanation of the key.
† Scale, from Latin word *scala*, meaning ladder.
‡ See Appendix V for the physicist's explanation of the major scale.
§ All chords whose spellings conform to a diatonic scale, are called *diatonic chords*.

EXERCISE 1. Be able to write on the staff the tonic, dominant, and subdominant triads for any given major key.

EXERCISE 2. Be able to derive any given major scale by spelling the tonic, dominant, and subdominant triads.

The major scale brought into being by this specific arrangement of three major triads has the following properties:

Distance in Steps		1	1	½	1	1	1	½	
Scale Degree	1	2		3	4	5	6	7	8
Name of Interval		M2	M2	m2	M2	M2	M2	m2	

The following table names and defines each scale degree:

Scale Degree	Name	Description
1	Tonic	Key tone; root of tonic triad
2	Supertonic	One step above the tonic
3	Mediant	In terms of scale degrees, midway between tonic and dominant
4	Subdominant	Root of chord a fifth below the tonic
5	Dominant	Root of chord a fifth above the tonic
6	Submediant	In terms of scale degrees, midway between tonic and subdominant
7	Leading tone	The third of the dominant triad, in half-step relation to the tonic. In the progression dominant to tonic, the leading tone possesses a tendency to rise to the tonic degree.

THE KEY SIGNATURE

The *key signature* is composed of either one sharp or one flat or a group of sharps or flats and is found at the beginning of each staff. Its position is directly after the clef sign. A new signature in the course of a composition is preceded by a double-bar. The notes which are affected by the key signature must conform to it throughout the composition, providing a new signature is not introduced.

The system of key signatures used to identify major and minor keys seems to be uniformly adopted by the composers around 1750, although the style of music

THE TONAL ELEMENTS

to which it was applied was easily seventy-five years old. The cause of the confusion in signatures before 1750 was unquestionably due to the fact that composers were reluctant to give up the older signature tradition. The pre-key signature came about through the transposition of a cantus firmus and its accompanying voices.*

Guido d'Arezzo, early 11th century teacher and theorist, devised a method of transposing church melodies so that the melodies remained in a singable range while being accompanied by additional vocal parts. Using our knowledge of the major scale and applying Guido's principle of transposition at the fifth below or above the original scale, notice the appearance of one accidental for each transposition.†

Increase in ♭'s			*Increase in ♯'s*
	cdefgabc		
		gabcdef♯g	f
b	fgab♭cdef		
		def♯gabc♯d	f, c
b, e	b♭cde♭fgab♭		
		abc♯def♯g♯a	f, c, g
b, e, a	e♭fga♭b♭cde♭		

If this process is continued, the sharps will appear on the staff in the order of f, c, g, d, a, e, and b.

The flats will appear on the staff in the order of b, e, a, d, g, c, and f.

This historical explanation reveals why the signature has a definite order in the grouping of the accidentals. For example, the key of e-major has four sharps and three naturals. The signature indicates that a major key has been transposed upwards four times at the interval of the fifth. The accidentals in the signature will appear in the order of each transposition, and for e-major they will be f♯, c♯, g♯, and d♯.

The key signature for any major key is composed of the different accidentals which are found in the tonic, dominant, and subdominant triads. The key signature for a-major is derived as follows:

---

* The melody selected as the basis for a contrapuntal composition is called a *cantus firmus*.

† See articles in a dictionary of music or a history of music on Guido's Hexachord. Observe the close agreement of Guido's Hexachord to the major scale.

Placing the accidentals in the order of sharps on the staff given above, the signature of a-major is

EXERCISE 3. Write the key signature (on treble clef and bass clef) for any major key.

THE MINOR KEY

Continuing the application of Rameau's belief that major and minor keys are established by chord progression, play Version I and Version II of *Nun Komm der Heiden Heiland.*

Nun komm der Heiden Heiland
Vers. I
Vers. II
J. S. Bach

Note that both versions leave one with the impression that A is the tonic. From this, further deductions may be drawn, as follows:

1. If A is the tonic, the triads built on A can be identified as tonic, those on D as subdominant, and those on E as dominant.
2. All the triads on the tonic and subdominant are minor. Three of the dominant triads are major, and one is minor.

When the tonic, subdominant, and dominant triads are all minor, as in the first measure of Version I, the notes included in these triads produce the **Natural Form** of the minor key.

The *Natural Minor Scale* is derived from the natural form of the minor key.

The natural minor scale has the following properties:

Step		1	½	1	1	½	1	1	
Scale Degree	1		2		3	4	5	6	7	8
Name of Interval		M2	m2	M2	M2	m2	M2	M2	

In Bach's use of the minor key, the dominant triad is generally major, especially when it precedes the tonic at the end of a phrase. When the tonic and the subdominant are minor triads and the dominant is a major triad, as in Version II, the notes of these triads constitute the Harmonic Form of the minor key.

Subdom.   Tonic   Dom.

The *Harmonic Minor Scale* is derived from the harmonic form of the minor key.

The harmonic minor scale has the following properties:

Step		1	½	1	1	½	1½	½	
Scale Degree	1		2		3	4	5	6	7	8
Name of Interval		M2	m2	M2	M2	m2	Aug. 2*	m2	

When the dominant triad is major, as in Version II, the third of the dominant triad, which is the seventh degree of the scale, requires an accidental. The seventh degree of the harmonic minor scale always requires an accidental on each occurrence, since it is not included in the signature.

The subdominant and the tonic are also sometimes made major by raising the third of the chord with an accidental. Let us observe the harmonic content of the following Bach chorale harmonization:

O wie selig seid ihr doch, ihr Frommen   J. S. Bach

3rd phrase

a   g   a   d   —   a

---

* The abbreviation for augmented second.

By using an ascending melodic line in the bass, Bach makes use of a major subdominant triad.

In the early 18th century style it was a customary procedure to end a composition which was in a minor key by the use of a tonic major triad.

Christ, unser Herr, zum Jordan kam

J. S. Bach

This practice of ending a minor composition with a triad containing a major third is called Tierce de Picardie. This practice appeared during the polyphonic era, and a decline in its usage began about 1750.

A summary of the foregoing discussion shows the harmonic content of a minor key as follows:

For example, key of g-minor

Subdominant   Tonic   Dominant

Accordingly, the possible tones used in g-minor, in scale form, are as follows:

If the tonic, subdominant, and dominant triads can all be major in a minor key, what is the difference between a major and a minor key? The author has found through research into this question that if the composer chooses to express himself in a minor key, he must use harmonic structures which are skillfully allocated in such a way as to maintain an aural effect of minor. This is a matter of frequency usage of harmonic material. Bach and his contemporaries use the available triads in a minor key as follows:

Tonic	minor triad	very frequent
	major triad	very infrequent
Dominant	major triad	very frequent
	minor triad	very infrequent

	minor triad	very frequent
Subdominant		
	major triad	infrequent

This table will control the auditory identification of the minor key. Composers, in order to maintain the conventional minor key, must use predominantly minor triads on the tonic and subdominant and a major triad on the dominant.

In the late 19th century and the 20th century, the natural minor scale was used more frequently, largely as a result of increased influence of folk music. In folk music the natural minor scale is generally more common than the harmonic minor scale.*

EXERCISE 4. Be able to write or play any natural minor scale.
EXERCISE 5. Be able to write or play any harmonic minor scale.

The tones in a minor key which are considered diatonic are found in the following harmonies: tonic minor, tonic major, subdominant minor, subdominant major, dominant major, and dominant minor triads.

Diatonic Tones of F-minor

A major key has seven diatonic tones, and a minor key has ten diatonic tones.

EXERCISE 6. Write or play the diatonic minor tones in scale form for any minor key.

The following table names and defines each diatonic scale degree in a minor key:†

Scale Degree	Name	Description
1	Tonic	Key tone; root of tonic triad
2	Supertonic	One step above the tonic
3	Mediant	In terms of scale degrees, midway between the tonic and dominant

---

* This subject will be taken up in Chapter 32.

† Considering the natural minor as the basis of the minor key, there are two mediants, two submediants, subtonic, and leading tone. The scale degrees which differ from the natural minor are defined as follows:

$\sharp$
3   raised-three

$\sharp$
6   raised-six

$\sharp$
7   raised-seven

For example, the tonic chord containing the Tierce de Picardie will be called tonic with raised-three and will be written I.

$\sharp$
3

Scale Degree	Name	Description
♯ 3	Raised mediant	Tierce de Picardie
4	Subdominant	Root of chord a fifth below the tonic
5	Dominant	Root of chord a fifth above the tonic
6	Submediant	In terms of scale degrees, midway between the tonic and subdominant
♯ 6	Raised submediant	Promotes a stepwise melodic line from the dominant up to the tonic
7	Subtonic	One step below the tonic
♯ 7	Leading tone	The third of the major dominant chord; in half-step relation to the tonic. As in major, this tone possesses a tendency to rise to the tonic.

MINOR KEY SIGNATURE

The key signature for any minor key is composed of the accidentals which are found in the Natural Minor. The accidentals are placed on the staff in the order of sharps or flats, depending on the key. For example, the key signature for e-flat is determined as follows:

There are six flats and one natural. The flats are placed on the staff in the order of flats.*

EXERCISE 7. Write the key signature (on treble clef and bass clef) for any minor key.

The *Harmonic Major Scale* based upon Rameau's concept is as follows:

* See order of flats, page 104.

EXERCISE 8. Be able to play in any major key the harmonic major scale.

The *Harmonic Minor Scale* based upon Rameau's concept is as follows:

EXERCISE 9. Be able to play in any minor key the harmonic minor scale.

Chapter 20

The Non-Harmonic Tones

From the time occidental music in the eleventh century adopted the harmonic concept,* two kinds of tones appear in a musical fabric. The tones which form the accepted harmonic elements of any period are called *Essential Tones.* All other tones in the musical fabric are *Unessential.*

In the 18th and 19th centuries the essential tone is a member of a chord, and it is called a *Harmonic Tone.* A *Non-Harmonic Tone* is one which is not found in the harmony, but is related stepwise to a tone in the harmony.

At 1 in the examples above, the non-harmonic tone is interpolated between two harmonic tones of the same harmony. At 2, two non-harmonic tones are interpolated between harmonic tones of the same harmony. At 3, two non-harmonic tones moving in contrary motion are found on the beat, and they are interpolated between harmonic tones of the same harmony. At 4 in the examples the non-harmonic tone is interpolated between harmonic tones which belong to different harmonies.

* The term *harmonic concept,* in its broader interpretation, is not limited to chords of three or more notes. An interval was considered as a harmony in the 11th, 12th, and 13th centuries.

A non-harmonic tone is attracted step-wise to a harmonic tone in somewhat the same manner as a piece of steel is attracted to a magnet. The following diagram illustrates the manner in which nine non-harmonic tones are attracted by the three tones of a major triad:

Interval	*Step*			*Step*	*Interval*

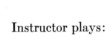  

```
                                      A♮      1       M2
                                  G   A♭      ½       m2
                           F#
   m2         ½

                                      F♮      ½       m2
                           E
   m2         ½     D#
                                      D♮      1       M2
                                  C   D♭      ½       m2
   m2         ½     B♮
   M2         1     B♭
```

EXERCISE 1. Singing the non-harmonic tones to any member of a major triad. The instructor plays a major triad and directs the student to sing one of the nine possible non-harmonic tones. The student sings the tone by approaching it through the root of the triad, following the chord line if necessary.

         Example: Sing a non-harmonic tone a half-step above the fifth of a major triad.

Instructor plays: Student responds:

EXERCISE 2. Resolve a given tone as a non-harmonic tone.

         The instructor plays any tone and directs the student to use it as a non-harmonic tone in a given relationship to the root, third, or fifth of a major triad. The student feels the chord tone a whole or half-step above or below, as the case may be, and sings the triad.

         Example: Resolve the non-harmonic tone f-sharp, which is a half-step below the third of a major third.

Instructor plays: Student responds: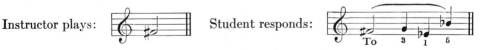

EXERCISE 3. Recognize the non-harmonic tones to a major triad. The instructor plays a major triad, following it with a non-harmonic tone. The student sings the non-harmonic tone and resolves it to a chord tone. The student then indicates the intervallic relationship to the chord tone.

Example:

Instructor plays: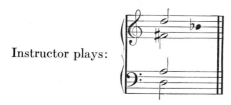

Student responds: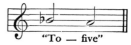

"To — five"

Student recites: A half-step above the fifth

A non-harmonic tone does not take the spelling of the harmonic tone to which it normally resolves. It uses the neighboring letter name. For example, a non-harmonic tone a half-step above the fifth of the e-flat major triad is c-flat.

EXERCISE 4. Spell a non-harmonic tone from dictation.
The instructor names and plays the major triad to which he plays non-harmonic tones. The student identifies each non-harmonic tone by reciting or writing the non-harmonic tone on staff paper.
Example: The e-flat major triad is given.

Instructor plays:

Student recites: f-sharp, d, a-flat, d-flat, etc.

Student writes:

At the completion of the study of non-harmonic tones to a major triad, study the relationship of non-harmonic tones to a minor triad, using in order the same exercises.*

CLASSIFICATION OF NON-HARMONIC TONES

In the course of a musical composition, non-harmonic tones are interpolated between harmonic tones. There are many ways in which the non-harmonic tone may be approached and left.

*See Appendix 6 for the relation of non-harmonic tones to a minor triad.

The first and last note at 1, 2, 3, and 4 are harmonic.   At 1, the non-harmonic tone 'g' is derived by step and left by step.   At 2, the non-harmonic tone is derived by step and left by leap.   At 3, the harmonic tone 'f' becomes a non-harmonic tone, due to the harmonic change.   The non-harmonic tone moves step-wise to the harmonic tone.   At 4, the non-harmonic tone is derived by step.   It then becomes the root of the new chord.   In this way, non-harmonic tones surrounded by harmonic tones tend to form short melodic figures, many of which become important in the evaluation of musical styles.

The manner in which the non-harmonic tone is derived and resolved will classify it.   Because of this, it is necessary to emphasize the importance of the classification of non-harmonic tones; for this is the basis of the concept of preparation and resolution of dissonance.

1. Passing Tone

When a non-harmonic tone is interpolated step-wise between two harmonic tones of different pitch, it is called a *passing tone.*

2. Suspension

If in a progression of two chords any of the tones of the first chord are delayed from their normal step-wise melodic movement at the moment the second chord appears, the non-harmonic dissonant effect is called a *suspension.*

3. Neighboring Tone

When a non-harmonic tone is interpolated step-wise between two harmonic tones of the same pitch, it is called a *neighboring tone.*

* Example (c) contains double passing tones.   The word *double* is always used in connection with the type non-harmonic tone if both non-harmonic tones are of the same type.   For example, double suspension, double lower neighboring tones, etc.

4. ANTICIPATION

If in a progression of two chords any of the tones of the first chord move step-wise to forecast the consonant intervals of the second chord, the dissonance is called an *anticipation*.

5. ESCAPE TONE

If a non-harmonic tone is derived step-wise and leaps to a harmonic tone, it is called an *escape tone*.

6. APPOGGIATURA

If a non-harmonic tone is derived by leap and resolved step-wise, it is called an *appoggiatura*.

7. Changing Tone

If a non-harmonic tone is derived step-wise and leaps an interval of a third in opposite direction to another non-harmonic tone which is resolved step-wise, the dissonant tones are called *changing tones*.

A non-harmonic tone which appears on an important pulsation is called *accented*. The following example illustrates an *accented passing tone*, an *accented appoggiatura*, and an *accented suspension*.*

EXERCISE 5. In the following examples, name each non-harmonic tone. The basic harmony is supplied on the third staff below the composition.

Sonata in F Major, first movement

W. Mozart

measure 24

Harmonic analysis

* The author prefers to call this an accented suspension because the melodic contour is the same as the suspension. Melodic contour then is one of the important elements in the definition of a non-harmonic tone.

Uns ist ein Kindlein heut' gebor'n

J. S. Bach

Harmonic analysis

Sonata, Op. 31, No. 3

L. von Beethoven

Harmonic analysis

etc.

The basic and most often used non-harmonic tone is the passing tone.   This is best illustrated in the melodic forms of both the major and minor scales

EXERCISE 6. Be able to play any melodic major scale with the accompanying tonic, dominant, and subdominant triads.

Melodic Minor Scale

EXERCISE 7. Be able to play any melodic minor scale with the accompanying tonic, dominant, and subdominant triads.

$\mathcal{C}$hapter 21

The Diminished Triad

The diminished triad appears in pre-18th century music as a structure composed of a minor third and a major sixth erected upon the same bass tone.

This sonority is found as far back as the late 14th and early 15th centuries.   Typical 15th century examples are these:

The structure arranged in thirds is composed of two minor thirds.

120

As in the study of the major and minor triads, the musical mind analyzes the sonority according to the following procedure:

The interval at (a) is a minor third. At (b) the interval which is composed of six tempered half-tones is called a diminished fifth. The inversion of a diminished fifth produces an interval which is likewise composed of six tempered half-tones. This interval is an augmented fourth. The two intervals, b-f and f-b, divide an octave into two equal parts. Although each interval is composed of six tempered half-tones, there is a harmonic difference between the two intervals. B-f contains a d which is equidistant from b and f. This tends to break b-f into six tempered half-tones. The early composers used the augmented fourth as a component part of a harmony. As a melodic interval it was avoided, and it was called the "Diabolus in Musica" (devil in music). They considered f-b as composed of three whole tones. F to g, g to a, and a to b are whole tones. The resulting aural effect is called the tritone. A diminished triad is classified as a dissonant chord containing the tritone.

The triad rarely appears with the root in the bass. Notice the continued preference for using the 15th century structure in the following 18th century examples:

SPELLING THE DIMINISHED TRIAD

To spell a diminished triad on any given root, spell the tone a minor third above the root, spell the tone a diminished fifth (lower the perfect fifth a half-step) above the root, and spell the triad in the order of the root, third, and fifth. For example, spell a d-diminished triad. A minor third above d is f; a diminished fifth above d is a-flat (the perfect fifth is a); the d-diminished triad spelling is d f a♭.

EXERCISE 1. Be able to spell any diminished triad.

EXERCISE 2. Place the diminished triad on the staff, considering each given tone as the root.

EXERCISE 3. Play the diminished triad, considering each given tone as the root.

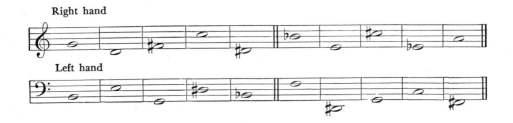

PLAYING THE DIMINISHED TRIAD

In keeping with the four-voice part-writing of the composers up to the 20th century, the diminished triad will be played only in its first inversion.* It is the common practice of the composers to double the third (the bass tone) in the first inversion of a diminished triad when writing in four voices. Out of 640 diminished triads in first inversion, the author found root doubled, 6; third doubled, 416; and the fifth doubled, 218. From this we may conclude that it is advisable at first to double the third of the first inversion of a diminished triad at the keyboard.

EXERCISE 4. Play the first inversion of any diminished triad in the position of either the octave, third, or fifth.
> Example: Play the first inversion of the f-sharp diminished triad in the position of the octave.

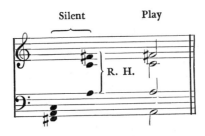

* The author has made an exhaustive study of the use of the diminished triad and presents the following facts: For example, in Bach's chorale harmonizations there are 681 diminished triads; 38, root in bass; 640, third in bass; and 3, fifth in bass. For examples of root in the bass, see *Contrapuntal Harmonic Technique of the 18th Century* by A. I. McHose, page 206, Example 446, and page 215, Example 464.

THE APPLICATION OF THE THEORY OF INVERSION

The diminished triad reacts to the theory of inversion in the same manner as the major and minor triads.*

EXERCISE 5. Be able to recognize the root of a diminished triad.
> Example: A series of diminished triads will be played. Listen to the triad and then sing the root, using a neutral syllable.†

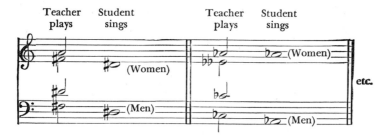

In the next exercises, follow the plan used in Exercise 8, Chapter 15.

EXERCISE 6. Identify the root, third, or fifth in the soprano of a diminished triad.

EXERCISE 7. Identify a major, minor, or diminished triad.
> Example: A phrase of music will be played. As the phrase is repeated, identify orally or in writing the type of each triad.
> When writing, use M for a major triad; m for a minor triad; d for a diminished triad.

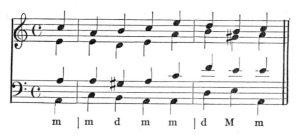

m | m   d   m   m | d   M   m

---

* Some theorists explain the diminished triad on the leading tone as an incomplete form of the dominant seventh chord. Since this reasoning, however, cannot be applied to other diminished triads, such as the supertonic triad in minor, the author prefers to consider all diminished triads as genuine and independent chords, and believes that analysis of music of the 18th and 19th centuries tends to support this view.

† Avoid dictating diminished triads in succession which have a common tone, since this makes it difficult to isolate the root of the second chord.

EXERCISE 8. Identify a major, minor, or diminished triad; in addition, give the soprano and bass of each triad.

        Example: A phrase of music will be played which contains major, minor, and diminished triads. As the phrase is repeated, identify the type triad and its soprano and bass.

The oral or written response is in terminology. The answer for the first three chords is as follows:

    1. first inversion of a minor triad in the position of the octave
    2. first inversion of a diminished triad in the position of the third
    3. minor triad in the position of the third

EXERCISE 9. Writing the diminished triad in four voices on the staff from dictation when the soprano is given.

        Example: The instructor names g-flat in the soprano and plays the first inversion of the c-diminished triad in the position of the fifth. The student's solution appears as follows:

For a series of chords, the student is given the soprano tones as follows:

EXERCISE 10. Describing a diminished triad from dictation when the soprano tone is known.

        Example: The instructor names d as the soprano tone.

Instructor plays:

Student recites or writes: the first inversion of the
d-diminished triad in the
position of the octave

EXERCISE 11. Describing major, minor, and diminished triads when the soprano is known.
Example: The soprano of a phrase of music is placed on the staff. The
instructor at the piano harmonizes the given soprano. The
student's response, by reciting or writing, describes the chord
used for each soprano tone.

Given soprano:*

Instructor plays:

Student responds: g-minor triad in the position of the third

first inversion of the f-sharp diminished triad in the
position of the third

first inversion of the g-minor triad in the position of
the octave

e-flat major triad in the position of the third

first inversion of the a-diminished triad in the position of the octave

d-major triad in the position of the third

g-minor triad in the position of the octave

PART-WRITING THE FIRST INVERSION
OF A DIMINISHED TRIAD

Although the third is most frequently doubled in the first inversion of a
diminished triad, doubling of either the root or the fifth is also encountered.

* The student must apply the principle of the key signature. Notes appearing on b and e will be understood
to be b-flat and e-flat.

The Doubled Third

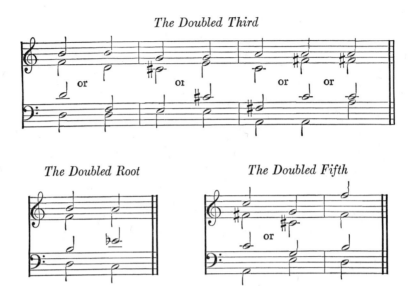

The Doubled Root   *The Doubled Fifth*

EXERCISE 12. Add the alto and tenor voices, complying with the indicated structure and doubling.

Doubling

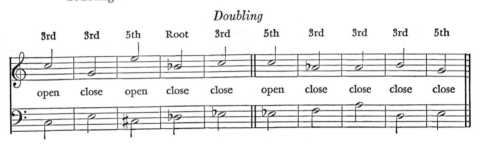

INTERVALS AND THE DIMINISHED TRIAD

The intervals which imply a diminished triad are listed in the following table:

Chord Members	Name of Interval
1 u 1 3 u 3 5 u 5 1 d 1 3 d 3 5 d 5	Perfect octave
1 u 5 5 d 1	Diminished fifth*

* See page 121.

Chord Members	Name of Interval
5 u 1 ⎫	
1 d 5 ⎭	Augmented fourth
1 u 3; 3 d 1	Minor third
3 u 5; 5 d 3	Minor third
3 u 1; 1 d 3	Major sixth
5 u 3; 3 d 5	Major sixth

The intervals of the major third, minor sixth, perfect fifth, and perfect fourth do not imply a diminished triad.

The procedure established in Exercises 1 and 2 of Chapter 16 is to be followed in the next two exercises.

EXERCISE 13. Playing intervallic relationships in the diminished triad.

EXERCISE 14. Sing any intervallic relationship from a given pitch based on a diminished triad.

Owing to the unusual intervallic structure of the diminished triad, namely, two minor thirds, two major sixths, and the ambiguous tritone, the harmonic background will be supplied during the process of interval dictation.

EXERCISE 15.* Recognize the chord members and name the interval based on a diminished triad.
The instructor, at the piano, plays an interval ascending or descending, based on a diminished triad. Identify the implied chord members and name the interval.
Example:

Instructor plays:

Student recites: 5 up to 1, augmented fourth

or

writes: 5 u 1, Aug. 4th

EXERCISE 16. The interval placed on the staff from dictation.
The instructor names the first note if the interval is to be played melodically, or the lowest note if the interval is to be played harmonically. After the interval is played, the student determines the chord members and writes the chord on the bass clef, then writes the second note. The name of the interval is placed directly below the written interval.
(For this exercise the harmonic background is a diminished triad.)

* When dictating the intervals harmonically, use the procedure of Exercise 4 of Chapter 16.

Example: The instructor names c-sharp.

Instructor plays: Student responds:

dim. 5th

EXERCISE 17. Recognize from dictation the following intervals: octave, perfect fifth, perfect fourth, diminished fifth,* augmented fourth,* major third, minor third, major sixth, and minor sixth.

The instructor names the first note of a melodic interval, or either upper or lower note of a harmonic interval. After the interval is played, the student writes only the interval on the staff and its name.

* The instructor plays the harmonic background when dictating the diminished fifth or augmented fourth.

Chapter 22

The Classification of Root Movement

In Chapter 19 we found that the successive roots of chords as they appeared in the course of a musical composition were either at the prime,* fifth, second, or third. At the time of Rameau these root movements were as follows:†

Interval	Frequency of Usage
fifth	58%
second	23%
third	10%
prime	9%

In addition to the fact that the roots of chords progress according to the above table, research shows that there is law and order in the movement of roots within a musical composition.

For the purposes of this study, all root movements of the compositions analyzed have been transposed to either D-major or d-minor. The research was conducted as follows:

ROOT MOVEMENT TO THE TONIC

1. The tonic chords were located.
2. The interval relation of the root of the preceding chord to the root of the tonic was tabulated.
3. The following was the result of the study:

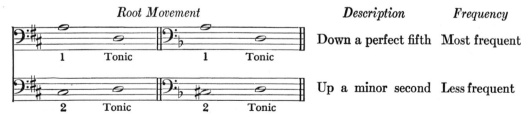

Root Movement	Description	Frequency
1 — Tonic / 1 — Tonic	Down a perfect fifth	Most frequent
2 — Tonic / 2 — Tonic	Up a minor second	Less frequent

* Prime, as used here, indicates that the root is repeated.

† The percentages are based on over five thousand successive chord progressions from complete compositions by Bach, Handel, Graun, and Telemann.

At 1, the root movement is dominant to tonic. At 2, the root movement is leading tone to tonic.

Chords built on either the dominant or leading tone progress normally to the tonic, and are called chords of the *first classification.*

The following example illustrates chords of the first classification progressing normally to the tonic:

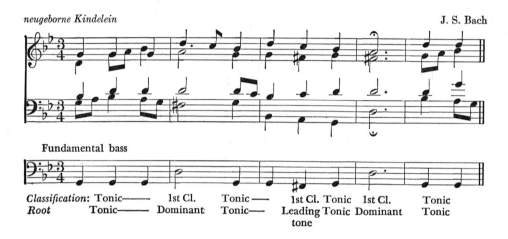

neugeborne Kindelein   J. S. Bach

Fundamental bass

Classification:	Tonic———	1st Cl.	Tonic ——	1st Cl.	Tonic	1st Cl.	Tonic
Root	Tonic———	Dominant	Tonic——	Leading tone	Tonic	Dominant	Tonic

Root Movement to the First Classification

1. The dominant and leading tone chords were located.
2. The interval relation of the root of the preceding chord to either the dominant or leading tone was tabulated.
3. The following was the result of the study:

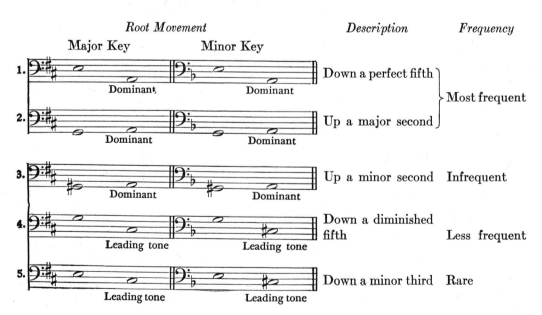

Root Movement		Description	Frequency
Major Key	Minor Key		
1. Dominant	Dominant	Down a perfect fifth	⎫ Most frequent
2. Dominant	Dominant	Up a major second	⎭
3. Dominant	Dominant	Up a minor second	Infrequent
4. Leading tone	Leading tone	Down a diminished fifth	Less frequent
5. Leading tone	Leading tone	Down a minor third	Rare

At 1, the root movement is supertonic to dominant.

At 5, the root movement is supertonic to leading tone.

At 2, the root movement is subdominant to dominant.

At 4, the root movement is subdominant to leading tone.

At 3, the root movement is raised-subdominant* to dominant.

Chords which have their roots on the subdominant or supertonic progress normally to chords of the first classification, and are called chords of the *second classification*.

The following example illustrates chords of the second classification progressing normally to chords of the first classification:

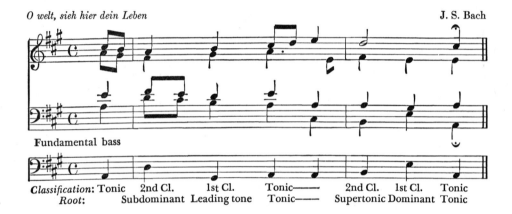

Root Movement to the Second Classification

1. The supertonic and subdominant chords were located.
2. The interval relation of the root of the preceding chord to either the supertonic or subdominant was tabulated.
3. The following was the result of the study:

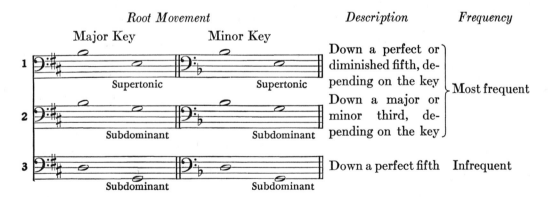

---

* The raised-subdominant is an altered tone. See Part I, Chapter 22 of *Contrapuntal Harmonic Technique of the 18th Century*, by A. I. McHose.

At 1, the root movement is submediant to supertonic.

At 2, the root movement is submediant to subdominant.

At 3, the root movement is tonic to subdominant. In this case the tonic chord must be a dissonance; in the Bach technique it is a seventh chord:

Chords which have their roots on the submediant, and dissonant chords which have their roots on the tonic, progress normally to chords of the second classification, and are called chords of the *third classification*.

The following example illustrates a chord of the third classification progressing normally to the chord of the second classification:

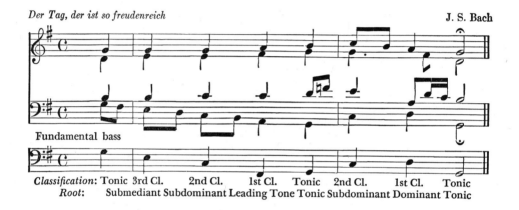

Der Tag, der ist so freudenreich   J. S. Bach

Classification:	Tonic	3rd Cl.	2nd Cl.	1st Cl.	Tonic	2nd Cl.	1st Cl.	Tonic
Root:	Submediant	Subdominant	Leading Tone	Tonic	Subdominant	Dominant	Tonic	

Root Movement to the Third Classification

1. The submediant and discords of the tonic were located.
2. The interval relation of the root of the preceding chord to either the submediant or tonic (root of a discord) was tabulated.
3. The following was the result of the study:

Root Movement		Description	Frequency
Major Key	Minor Key	Down a perfect fifth	Nothing with which to compare this root movement
Submediant	Submediant		

In the example above, chords which have their roots on the mediant progress normally to chords of the third classification and are called chords of the *fourth classification*.

From this discussion, it is apparent that a chord of the fourth classification is the most remote from the tonic, and a chord of the first classification is nearest to the tonic. Through analysis it is found that chords of any classification tend to progress to chords of the next lower number classification, and so on until the tonic chord is reached. This kind of chord harmonic movement is called a *Normal Progression*. The following table illustrates the normal progression:

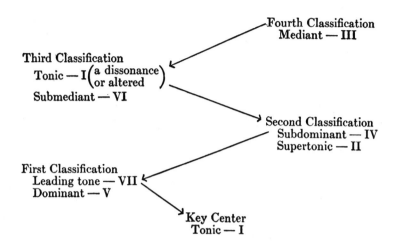

The Roman numeral to the right of each functional name is used in analysis; it is a symbol to represent the function of the chord.

There are four basic ways in which to leave a chord, namely, by normal progression, repetition, elision, and retrogression.

Functions which are most often repeated are:—first, tonic; second, dominant; third, subdominant; and fourth, supertonic. The remaining functions are rarely repeated. The following example illustrates repetition:

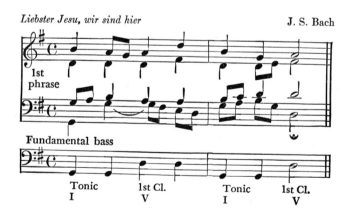

If a chord of the third classification progresses to a chord of the first classification, the progression is called an *elision*. The common elisions are as follows:

Fourth classification to second classification: mediant to subdominant
Third classification to first classification: submediant to dominant
Second classification to tonic: subdominant to tonic

The following examples illustrate elision:

At 1 and 2, the VI progresses to V, eliding the second classification chord II or IV.

Thus far the roots of the chords which were not tonic have progressed in one direction: a chord of the fourth classification progressed normally to a chord of the third classification, and so on; and in the elision the progression has always been toward the tonic center. Occasionally, however, composers interrupt this type of movement by progressing to a more remote classification; for example, a first classification dominant chord may progress to a second classification supertonic. This movement away from the tonic is called *retrogression*. Common retrogressions are:

> submediant to mediant
> dominant to supertonic
> dominant to subdominant

The less common retrogressions are as follows:

> dominant to mediant
> subdominant to submediant
> supertonic to submediant

The following examples illustrate retrogression:

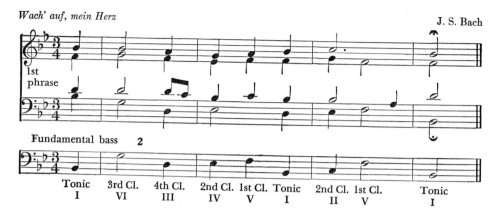

Wach' auf, mein Herz   J. S. Bach

	Tonic	3rd Cl.	4th Cl.	2nd Cl.	1st Cl.	Tonic	2nd Cl.	1st Cl.	Tonic
	I	VI	III	IV	V	I	II	V	I

At 1, a retrogression V to IV occurs, but the movement immediately swings back to a normal progression IV to V.

At 2, a retrogression VI to III occurs, but the movement immediately swings back in the elision III to IV which in turn progresses normally to V.

Using the same compositions containing over five thousand successive chord progressions, we find that Bach, Handel, Graun, and Telemann use normal progression, repetition, elision, and retrogression as follows:

	Bach	Handel	Graun	Telemann	Average
Normal progression...........	76%	82%	82%	79%	79%
Repetition..................	14	6	8	10	10
Retrogression...............	6	9	5	7	7
Elision....................	4	3	5	4	4

Continuing the analysis of the compositions, the frequency usage of the classifications is:

	Bach	Handel	Graun	Telemann	Average
Tonic......................	38%	42%	40%	35%	39%
First Classification...........	34	34	34	38	35
Second Classification.........	19	18	18	18	18
Third Classification..........	7	5	7	6	6
Fourth Classification.........	2	1	1	3	2

It is not the author's intention that the student memorize percentages. These percentages, however, support the explanation of the fundamental principles which control the key center. The student can make simple deductions concerning musical devices which make up the basis of 18th and 19th century composition. The frequency of usage studies presented in this chapter serve as a guide in the presentation of many of the remaining chapters.

QUESTIONS

1. In a succession of chords, what interval is most frequent in the fundamental bass?
2. What interval is least frequent in the fundamental bass?
3. Name, in descending order of usage, the harmonic functions which are most often repeated.
4. What are the four basic ways by which a chord may be left?
5. Which of these ways has the highest average frequency?
6. Name at least two common retrogressions.
7. Name at least two common elisions.
8. Of the classifications of harmonic functions, which has the highest frequency of usage?
9. Which of the classifications has the lowest frequency in usage?
10. In your own words, describe the method used to determine the classification of harmonic movement.

Chapter 23

The Tonic

The manner in which composers use the tonic harmony is of utmost importance. The fact that the tonic chord is preceded by chords of the first classification has been established. The tonic chord has two other important uses, which are as follows:

1. The tonic chord may progress to any chord in its key.
2. The tonic chord may be used between two chords which form a normal progression without disturbing their classification.

In the following examples the chorale phrases open with the tonic chord and progress to chords which have their roots in different classifications:

In the following example the tonic triad appears between the third classification and the second classification, and between the second classification and the first classification:

137

Was Gott thut, das ist wohlgethan   *Was mein Gott will, das g'scheh' allzeit*   J. S. Bach

At 1, the IV progresses to I, which in turn progresses to V. The I in no way disturbs the normal feeling that the IV actually progresses to the V.

At 2, the VI actually progresses to IV, and the I in no way disturbs the normal progression of the third classification chord. The same is true in connection with IV at 3, which actually progresses to V.

Characteristics:

     a. The tonic chord is the chord of rest.

     b. It is the harmony which identifies the key.

     c. It may appear at any point within the phrase.

The tonic chord appears in major and minor keys, as follows:

Major Key		*Minor Key*	
Symbol	*Type Chord*	*Symbol*	*Type Chord*
I	Major Triad	I	Minor Triad
		I$_{\#3}$	Major Triad (only as last chord of the phrase)

HARMONIC DICTATION

The process of identifying the functions of a key when music is played is called harmonic dictation.

Drill: A phrase of music will be played once. At its completion, sing the tonic triad.

Instructor plays:

Student sings:

"Loo" - - - -

Drill: A phrase will be played twice. As it is repeated, sing the tonic triad each time it appears.

Instructor plays:

Student sings on
a neutral syllable:

Drill: A phrase will be played twice. As it is repeated, recite, at each appearance of the tonic, either "major tonic" or "minor tonic," as the case may be.

Instructor plays:

Student recites:

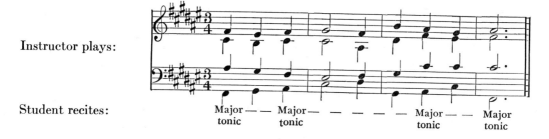

Drill:

Instructor plays:

Student recites:

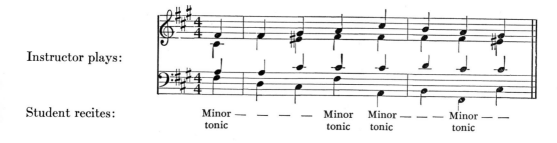

Drill: A phrase will be played twice. As it is repeated, identify the tonic triad as it appears by writing the Roman numeral I. The remaining chords should be represented by dashes.

Instructor plays:

Student recites: I, | I,   −,   −, | I,   I, |−,   −, | I

MELODIC DICTATION

The process of reproducing in musical notation a melody which has been played is called melodic dictation. Melodic dictation is not a drill in a series of abstract intervals. The melodies which will be played are based on only one chord, namely, the tonic. From the study of the triad and the intervals locked up in the triad, it will be possible to analyze at any point of a dictated melody just what the harmonic value is of the tone which is to be symbolized. The next example gives, first, a melody which was dictated, and second, the student's solution and analysis which shows how the tones were heard.

The dictation exercise:

The student's solution:

EXERCISE:* The procedure for performing melodic dictation is as follows:

1. The instructor will give the name of the first note.
2. The melody will be played twice. Determine the key and meter, and prepare the staff.
3. The melody will be played once.†
    a. Making the conductor's beat, sing the melody on a neutral syllable.
    b. Place the notation on the staff.
    c. Make a complete harmonic analysis.
4. The exercise will be played once more to check your solution.

   * Melodic dictation exercises are found in the *Teachers Dictation Manual*, page 23.

   † If the exercise has more than one phrase, the first phrase will be played and time will be given to write the notation; then the first and second phrases will be played. The second phrase will be repeated.

Chapter 24

Triads in the First Classification: Dominant and Leading Tone

The diatonic triads which are found in the first classification of major and minor keys are as follows:

Triads in the First Classification

Major Key

Name	Symbol	Type Chord
Dominant	V	Major Triad
Leading Tone	VII	Diminished Triad

Minor Key

Name	Symbol	Type Chord
Dominant with raised-seven	V #7	Major Triad
Dominant (infrequent)	V	Minor Triad
Leading Tone with raised-seven	VII #7	Diminished Triad

The following examples illustrate the use of these triads in a variety of musical textural styles during the 18th and 19th centuries:

Warum betrübst du dich   *Nun komm der Heiden Heiland*   J. S. Bach

Kom, heiliger Geist   G. Telemann

Der Tod Jesu, No. 6   C. H. Graun

Rondo from Sonata in C (K 205ᵇ)   M. Mozart

Rondo for Piano   J. Hummel

KEYBOARD AND PART-WRITING

The chord progression at the close of a phrase is called a *cadence*.   Chords of the first classification play an important rôle in the cadence.

Example:

The normal progression of a first-classification chord to tonic at the close of a phrase is called an *Authentic Cadence*.

Example:

The *perfect authentic cadence* is a special cadence in which both the dominant and tonic chords have their roots in the bass and the soprano ascends or descends stepwise to the root of the tonic.

Example:

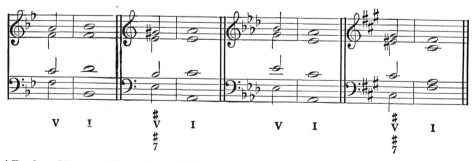

* For figured bass symbols, see Appendix I.

The perfect authentic cadence uses the two most fundamental principles of four-voice part-writing. Establishing the usual practice that a major or minor triad written in four voices must have two roots, a third and a fifth, the *first conventional method* of connecting two triads with their roots a fifth apart is as follows:

When one triad progresses to another which has its root a fifth above or below the first, keep the common tone in the same voice and move the remaining voices stepwise to the nearest notes of the following triad. Both chords must remain in the same structure.

Example:

Part-write the following perfect authentic cadences, harmonizing scale tones 7–8 or #7–8.

EXERCISE 1:

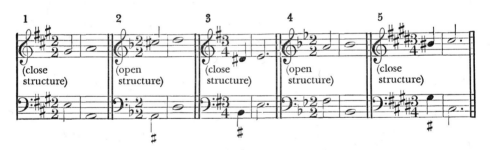

Play at the keyboard, using the same principles of part-writing, the following perfect authentic cadences:

EXERCISE 2:

The *second conventional method* is as follows:

When one triad progresses to another which has its root a fifth above or below the first, the three upper voices move in similar motion to the next triad tone. Both chords must remain in the same structure.

Example:

V   I   V   I
                7
                ♯

Part-write the following perfect authentic cadences, harmonizing scale tones 2–1:
EXERCISE 3:

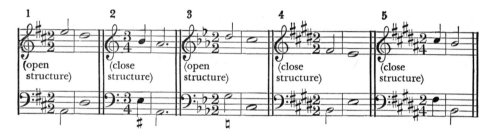

EXERCISE 4:

EXERCISE 5. Be able to part-write or play at the keyboard a perfect authentic cadence in any major or minor key.

The *imperfect authentic cadence* is an authentic cadence which has the third or fifth in the soprano of the tonic triad. It may also have the first-class chord, either V or VII, in first inversion. When the V and I have their roots in the bass, the imperfect authentic cadences use either the first or second conventional part-writing method.

Part-write the following imperfect authentic cadences, harmonizing scale tones 2–3, 5–3, and 5–5:

Play the following imperfect authentic cadences:

EXERCISE 6. Be able to play an imperfect authentic cadence in any key, using the root in the bass on V and I.

The first inversion of the V progressing to I may be used as an imperfect authentic cadence.

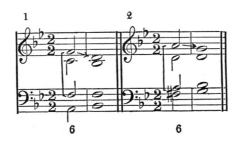

At 1 and 2, the first inversion of the V has the soprano tone doubled; and the I has two roots, a third and a fifth.* At 1, the doubled interval of the chord is left by oblique motion; that is, the tenor f remains the same, and the soprano f descends to the d. At 2, the doubled interval of the chord is left by contrary motion, the tenor a rises to the b-flat, and the soprano a descends to g.

In the first inversion of a triad, double the soprano. Oblique or contrary motion should be used in leaving the doubled interval in the chord progression of the inversion of a triad or a triad with the root in the bass.

* See Chapter 15, page 80.

Part-write the following imperfect authentic cadences, harmonizing scale tones 2–1, 5–3, and 5–5.

EXERCISE 7:

Play the following imperfect authentic cadences.

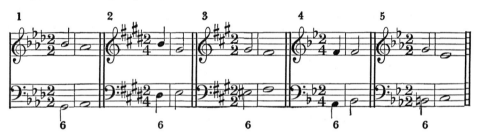

The progression, first inversion of VII to I harmonizing the scale tones 7–8 at the close of a phrase, is an imperfect authentic cadence.

Example:

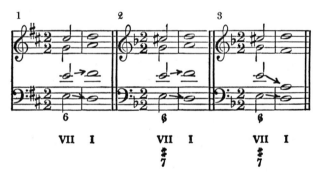

At 1, 2, and 3, the first inversion of the VII has the bass doubled, the third of the diminished triad; and the root position of I has two roots, a third and a fifth.* At 1 and 2, the doubled tones are left by contrary motion. At 3, the doubled tones are left by similar motion. The tenor a descends a fifth, so that the d-minor triad has two roots, a third and a fifth.

Part-write the following imperfect authentic cadences, using the first inversion of VII

to I and the scale steps 7–8 or 7–8.

* See Chapter 21, page 122.

EXERCISE 8:

Play the following imperfect authentic cadences:

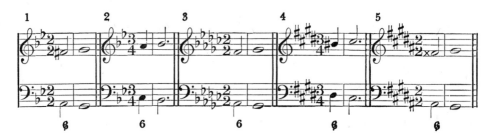

EXERCISE 9. Be able to play an imperfect authentic cadence in any key, using the first inversion of VII–I harmonizing the scale tones 7–8 or 7–8.

The progression of the tonic to the dominant at the close of a phrase is called a *half-cadence*.

Example:

Part-write the following half-cadences:

Play at the keyboard the following half-cadences:

EXERCISE 10. Be able to play a half-cadence in any major or minor key.

HARMONIC DICTATION*

Drill: A phrase will be played twice. As it is repeated, sing the root of each chord.

Instructor plays:

You sing on a neutral syllable:

Drill: A phrase will be played twice. As it is repeated, identify orally or in writing the
type of each chord.

M = Major triad
m = minor triad
d = diminished triad

Instructor plays:

You recite or write: m   d   m   M | m   m   M

Drill: While you are singing the root of each chord in an exercise, the instructor may halt
the phrase at any point. Sing the root of the chord to which you believe the last
chord should progress.

Note. If the root of the chord at the point at which the phrase was halted wants to
progress to the root of the tonic chord, the chord belongs to the first classification.

* Harmonic dictation exercises are found in the *Teachers Dictation Manual*, pages 52 and 53.

Instructor plays:

You sing:

The previous drill establishes the normal progression for the chords of the first classification.   A chord which has its root on the dominant or leading tone, normally progresses to the tonic.

Drill: A phrase is played twice.   As it is repeated, recite or write the classification of each chord.

I = Tonic

1st Cl. = First Classification

Instructor plays:

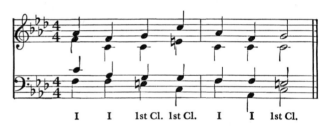

You recite or write: I   I   1st Cl. 1st Cl.   I   I   1st Cl.

As a phrase is played,* recite or write the name of each chord.

Instructor plays:

You recite or write: I | V   I   V   I | VII   I   V

MELODIC ANALYSIS AND SIGHT-SINGING

In this and subsequent chapters, melodic analysis is focused upon laying a foundation for performance in sight-singing, melodic dictation, and melodic harmonization.   Philippe Rameau, in his treatises, refers to the fact that a melody constantly implies a harmonic background.   This fact has been presented earlier in this text, especially in Chapter 15.

* The instructor should play the phrase at least three times when the student is asked to write the symbols.

Melodic analysis is concerned not only with the harmonic implications of a melody. The form, tempo, and rhythmic organization of the tones of the melody are also important analytical factors. In Appendix II musical terms which characterize tempo are defined. Appendix III contains a brief discussion on form. The student should use these appendices for definitions, explanations, etc., when necessary.

Of the three functions, namely, I, V, and VII, the I as the tonal center and the V as a first-classification chord are the most natural; that is, they express themselves first in one's musical mind. The VII is a chord which is synthesized by the musical mind and, consequently, it expresses itself as a derived sonority in the first classification in the field of creative musical thinking. In melodic analysis and sight-singing it is doubtful whether one hears an implied VII. The VII is a chord in the vocabulary of the composer.

The steps leading to melodic analysis are as follows:

1. The melody is to be played a number of times.
2. Determine the form of the entire melody and classify the structure of each phrase.
3. Determine the implied natural harmonic background as suggested by the harmonic tones. Place the implied chords on a second staff beneath the given melody. Beneath these two staves give the functional analysis in terms of the Roman numerals.
4. Identify and name each non-harmonic tone. Use the following abbreviations:

> PT   = passing tone
> LNT = lower neighboring tone
> UNT = upper neighboring tone
> S   = suspension

> APP = appoggiatura
> ET   = escape tone
> Ant = anticipation

When a non-harmonic tone appears on an accent, prefix the type non-harmonic tone with A; for example:

> accented passing tone   = A–PT
> accented suspension   = A–S
> accented upper neighboring tone = A–UNT

The following example illustrates the manner in which a melody is to be analyzed.

The melody is a period. The first phrase has a feminine beginning with a masculine cadence. The second phrase is in the same form.

Analyze the following melodies:

Consécration à Marie — French Folksong
4. Poco lento

La bienheureuse Germaine cousine — France
5 Moderato

Burmand holder i Felten ud — Danish Folk Tune
6 Allegretto

Le roi Dagobert — France
7 Allegro

Hr. Peder han hande en Datter saa vaen　　　　　Danish Folk Melody

8　　　*Andantino*

SIGHT-SINGING

Musical pedagogical tradition has established sight-singing as one of the important contributing skills in the development of a musician. The ability to reproduce at first sight the musical meaning of a melodic line can be acquired by perseverance. There is more truth than fiction in the trite statement that sight-singing is acquired only by sight-singing. Development in achieving this skill, however, should always be in proportion to acquired musical knowledge. Rhythmic drills and melodic analysis are a necessary prerequisite to sight-singing. The melodies which are to be sung at sight in this text do not contain rhythmic, formal, or harmonic backgrounds which have not been presented.

Sight-singing procedure is as follows:

1. Scan the melody which is to be sung at sight, to determine tempo and key.
2. Either the octave position of the tonic chord or the first note of the melody will be played to introduce the melody.
3. Making the conductor's beat, sing the melody, using the letter names for each note. When the note has a sharp or a flat before it, sing only the letter name and *think* the sharp or flat.

Examples:

Je crois en Dieu le Père tout puissant　　　　　French Folksong

1　　　*Allegro moderato*

La mission est ouverte　　　　　French Folksong

2　　　*Lento*

THEMES FROM 18TH AND 19TH CENTURY COMPOSERS

Quartet in A minor, Op. 132, fifth movement   L. von Beethoven

Allegro appassionato

Trio in B, Op. 8, second movement, first theme   J. Brahms

Allegro molto

Concerto No. 2, Op. 40, for Piano. Introduction   F. Mendelssohn

Allegro appassionato

Overture: Fingal's Cave, Op. 26, second theme   F. Mendelssohn

Allegro moderato

Symphony No. 3, "Scotch," fourth movement, second theme   F. Mendelssohn

Vivacissimo

Overture, Le Domino noir, first theme   D. Auber

Allegretto

Brandenburg Concerto, No. 6, third movement   J. S. Bach

♩. = 80

Concerto No. 1 (3 Pianofortes and Orchestra), third movement   J. S. Bach

♩ = 72

Symphony No. 29 (K 201), first movement   W. Mozart

Allegro moderato

M. Cherubini

MELODIC DICTATION*

The procedure for performing melodic dictation is as follows:

1. The instructor will give the name of the first note.
2. The melody will be played twice. Determine the key and meter, and prepare the staff.
3. The melody will be played once.
   - *a.* Making the conductor's beat, sing the melody on a neutral syllable.
   - *b.* Place the notation on the staff.
   - *c.* Make a complete harmonic analysis.
4. The exercise will be played once more to check your solution.

PART-WRITING AND KEYBOARD DRILLS

Part-writing procedure for the root position of a triad is as follows:

1. A triad is to have two roots, a third and a fifth.
2. Change from open structure to close structure, or the reverse, may take place when a chord is repeated.
3. When a triad progresses to another which has its root a fifth away, it will be necessary to determine whether the first conventional method or the second conventional method promotes the best voice leading.

Part-write the following exercises:

* Melodic dictation exercises are found in the *Teachers Dictation Manual*, pages 24 and 25.

FIRST INVERSION OF I AND V

Part-writing procedures for the first inversion of I and V are as follows:

1. The best tone to double in I is the soprano; next best is the bass; last, the inner voices.   The best tone to double in V is the soprano; next inner voices; do not double the bass.   See (3).
2. Leave the doubled tones by contrary or oblique motion, and resort to similar motion only when the first two are impossible.
3. The leading tone is not doubled.
4. In this style, avoid parallel octaves, unisons, and fifths.

Part-write the following exercises:

THE FIRST INVERSION OF VII

The best tone to double in the first inversion of the **VII** is the bass. Occasionally the fifth is doubled in the first inversion of the **VII** in the position of the fifth. Keeping this in mind, use the same part-writing procedure in leaving the doubled tone.

Part-write the following:

MELODIC COMPOSITION

Before embarking upon the actual composition of a melody, one may find that a knowledge of the horizontal tendencies of the diatonic tones of a key center is useful. The rest tones or inactive tones of any key are those which constitute the tonic triad. All other tones in the center are active, and they possess the tendency to move stepwise to the nearest inactive tone.

Example:

Example:

In the last example, the second degree may rise or fall. The imperfect authentic cadence with the soprano line 2–3 is a very good example; likewise, the second degree as a passing tone, approached from the first degree and rising to the third degree in a tonic harmonic background. In like manner, the fourth degree as a passing tone approached from the third degree may ascend to the fifth degree.

The sixth degree as a passing tone in a dominant triad background may rise to the seventh degree, especially if it is approached from the fifth degree.

An inactive tone becomes temporarily active if it is used as a non-harmonic tone. Harmonic background may turn an inactive tone into an active tone, as follows:

In melodic composition unity within a phrase is achieved by the use of repetition, sequence, rhythmic repetition, and modified repetition or sequence.

Repetition is an exact restatement, upon the same scale-steps, of a group or figure.

Sequence is a restatement of a group or figure upon other scale-steps.

Third Symphony   L. von Beethoven
Allegro molto

False sequence is a restatement of a group or figure which shows partial adherence to sequence and partial adherence to repetition.

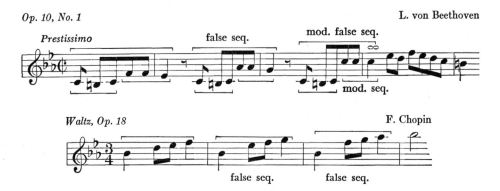

Op. 10, No. 1   L. von Beethoven

Waltz, Op. 18   F. Chopin

When the time values of a group or figure remain the same but the tones are varied, the device is *rhythmic repetition*.

Symphony in A   J. Haydn

Modified repetition or *modified sequence* retains the basic characteristics of the first statement of the group or figure; but in the restatement one or more intermediate tones may be added, or certain tones of the first statement may be omitted.

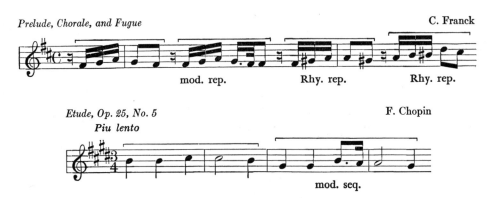

Prelude, Chorale, and Fugue   C. Franck

Etude, Op. 25, No. 5   F. Chopin
Piu lento

The writing of the original melody will be based on the tonic and dominant harmonies, and it is to be one phrase in length. The four types of phrases may be used.* The phrase may end in either an authentic cadence or a half-cadence. It is advisable at first to restrict the number of different harmonic backgrounds to two per measure, and one harmonic background is preferable. This point of view is, however, controlled by tempo. The following example illustrates a few possible ways in which a given melodic grouping may be expanded into a phrase.

EXERCISE 11. Develop into a phrase the following melodic groupings. Write at least two solutions to each melodic grouping:

* Use as a reference Appendix 3.

FOUR-VOICE SETTING OF A MELODY

The process of harmonizing a melody can be approached systematically without destroying one's artistic desires and aims. The following plan will be used:

1. Analyze the musical form of the melody to be harmonized
2. Chord choice:
   a. Work out the cadence formula
   b. Complete the harmonic scheme of the phrase leading to cadence formula
3. Compose the bass line to the melody in accord with the harmonies selected
4. Fill in the alto and tenor

Through melodic analysis, sight-singing, and melodic dictation drills, knowledge of the types of phrases has been established. In like manner the types of cadences, involving the tonic and triads of the first classification, have been presented. In this lesson chord choice will be limited to the selection and part-writing of the cadence.

Exercise 12. Select and part-write the cadence formula for the following phrase melodies:

Note: In 9 and 10 the non-harmonic tones will not disturb the normal bass, tenor, and alto voice leading.

Chapter 25

Triads in the Second Classification: Supertonic and Subdominant

The diatonic triads which are found in the second classification of major and minor keys are as follows:

Triads in the Second Classification

Major Key

Name	Symbol	Type Chord
Supertonic	II	Minor Triad
Subdominant	IV	Major Triad

Minor Key

Name	Symbol	Type Chord
Supertonic	II	Diminished Triad
Subdominant	IV	Minor Triad
Supertonic with raised six	II$\sharp\atop 6$	Minor Triad
Subdominant with raised six	IV$\sharp\atop 6$	Major Triad

The following examples illustrate the use of these triads in a variety of musical textural styles during the 18th and 19th centuries:

PART-WRITING AND KEYBOARD

An important but less used cadence is the plagal cadence, subdominant to tonic. The perfect plagal cadence is as follows:

The imperfect plagal cadence is as follows:

Before part-writing, determine the key and type of plagal cadence used in the following examples:

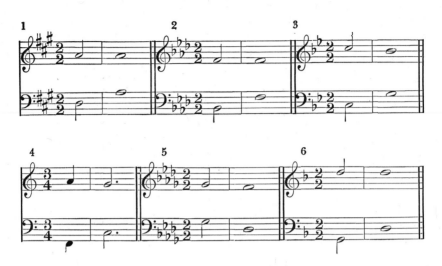

Play at the keyboard the following plagal cadences:

Exercise 1. Be able to play a perfect plagal or imperfect plagal cadence in any major or
minor key.

The normal progression of the subdominant triad is to the dominant triad.
The roots of these chords are a second apart.   Likewise, there are no tones common
to the two triads.   A *foreign* progression is one in which the two chords involved
have no tones in common.   Under these conditions the root of the second chord
may be either a step above or below that of the first chord.   The conventional
part-writing method is:

When a triad progresses to a triad which has its roots a second above or below,
the three upper voices move contrary to the bass.

Part-write the foreign progression IV, V, I.

Play at the keyboard, using the same part-writing principles, the following:

EXERCISE 2. Be able to play IV, V, I in any major or minor key.

Another normal progression, but less used, is the subdominant to the first inversion of the leading tone triad.   This progression is especially useful in harmonizing scale degrees 6–7–8 in major and 6–7–8 in minor.   Analyze the voice leading in the following examples:

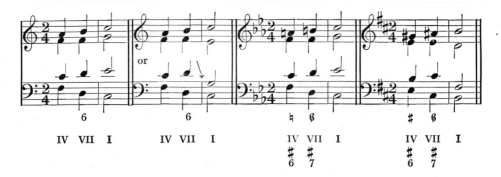

Part-writing:

Play at the keyboard:

The normal progression II–V, which involves roots a fifth apart, uses the first and second conventional part-writing methods. The supertonic triad is found most often in the position of the root or third. The position of the fifth is rarely encountered.

Example:

The progressions at 1 and 2 are most often used. The progression at 3 is not too frequent, and the progression at 4 is least often used.

Part-writing:

Play at the keyboard:

EXERCISE 3. Be able to play II–V–I in any major key.

The normal progression in major and minor of the first inversion of the super-tonic in either the position of the octave or the third is frequent. In both, the first inversion of the minor or diminished triads, the root or the third may be doubled. Study the voice leading from the first inversion of the supertonic triad in the following examples:

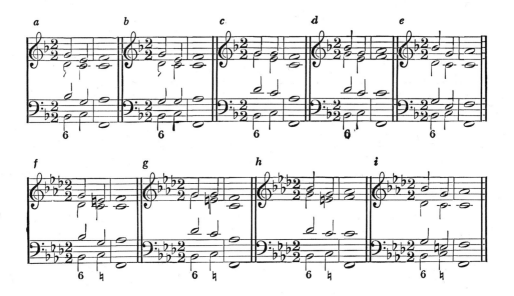

Part-writing:

Keyboard:

Be able to play the first inversion of II to V–I in any major or minor key.

HARMONIC DICTATION*

Characteristics:

> *a.* The triad in the second classification progresses normally to chords of the first classification.
>
> *b.* Its roots are either on the supertonic or the subdominant.

The harmonic dictation drills will be in the same order as those practised in Chapter 24.

Drill: A phrase will be played twice. As it is repeated, sing the root of each chord.

Drill: A phrase will be played twice. As it is repeated, identify orally or in writing the type of each chord.

Drill: While you are singing the root of each chord in an exercise, the instructor may halt the phrase at any point. Sing the root of the chord to which you believe the last chord should progress.

* The exercises for this section are found in the *Teachers Dictation Manual,* pages 53 through 68.

Note: If the root of the chord at the point at which the phrase was halted wants to progress to the root of a chord in the first classification, the chord belongs to the second classification.

Example:

Instructor plays:

Student sings:

The previous drill establishes the normal progression for the chords of the second classification. A chord which has its root on the supertonic or subdominant normally progresses to chords in the first classification. A tonic chord may appear between the normal progression of a second-classification chord to a first classification.

Drill: A phrase is played twice. As it is repeated, recite or write the classification of each chord.

I Tonic
1st Cl. First Classification
2nd Cl. Second Classification

Drill: As a phrase is played, recite or write the name of each chord.

THE ELISION AND RETROGRESSION OF THE FIRST AND SECOND CLASSIFICATION

To recognize the function of a chord, you have used the process of the normal progression. The nature of the tonic harmony to progress normally to any chord in its key, or to appear between the second and first classification, has been presented. It has been established that within the first classification the VII may progress to the V, and in the second classification the IV may progress to the II. However, the subject of harmonic movement is not complete without the process of elision and retrogression.* The retrogression V to II or IV occasionally appears in music, but the elision of IV to I is practically limited to the plagal cadence, especially in the early eighteenth century.

* Review definitions and explanation in Chapter 22.

Drill: As a phrase is played, sing the root of each chord.

Drill: A phrase will be played twice. As it is repeated, recite or write the character of the harmonic movement.

Recite	*Write*
Normal progression	N.
Repetition	Rep.
Retrogression	Ret.
Elision	E.

Note: When the tonic chord appears between harmonic movement which is not the normal progression, first classification to tonic, analyze the harmonic movement of the chord before the tonic to the chord after the tonic. For example, in the progression IV I V, the classification analysis ignores the tonic and considers the progression IV and V as a normal progression.

Example:

Instructor plays:

Student recites or writes:

(I)

N , N , Rep , N , Rep , **N**

Example:

Instructor plays:

Student recites or writes:

N , Ret , N , N , N , N

Drill: As a phrase is played at least three times, recite or write the name of each chord.

Instructor plays:

Student recites or writes:

I   V   IV   V   I   II   V

SOPRANO ON THE STAFF AND ROMAN NUMERALS

The first step in writing all voices from dictation is to place the soprano on the staff. The procedure which enables you to place the soprano on the staff and identify the chords is as follows:

Example:
    a. The instructor announces the key of the exercise.
    b. The instructor plays the exercise once.

    c. The student prepares the staff and determines the meter.

    d. The instructor repeats the exercise. The student identifies the chords. The solution should appear:

    e. The instructor repeats the exercise. The student places the soprano on the staff. The completed exercise should appear as follows:

ROMAN NUMERALS, SOPRANO, AND FIGURED BASS
ON THE STAFF

Drill: As a phrase is played, sing the bass melody on a neutral syllable.
　　Example:

Instructor plays:

Student sings on a
　neutral syllable:

Drill: The instructor gives the key of the exercise.　As the phrase is played, sing the bass
　　melody with the correct pitch names.
　　Example:

Instructor plays:

Student sings:

Drill: As a phrase of music is played, identify the position in the bass of each chord.
　　　　　　　R—Root position
　　　　　1st inv.—First inversion
　　　　　2nd inv.—Second inversion
　　Example:

Instructor plays:

Student recites or writes:

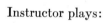

R ,　1st inv. , 1st inv. , R ,　　R ,　　R ,　　R

Drill: The instructor gives the key; you are to write the chord symbols, the soprano, and
　　the figured bass on the staff.

Example: The instructor announces the key of G minor.
        First step: You prepare the staff as follows:

Second step: The instructor plays the exercise.   You determine the meter.

Instructor plays:

Student adds meter and bars:

Third step: The instructor repeats the exercise.   You write the Roman
              numerals.

Student's solution thus far:

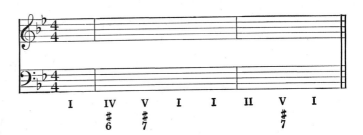

Fourth step: The instructor repeats the exercise.   You place the soprano
             on the staff.

Student's solution thus far:

Fifth step: The instructor repeats the exercise.   You place the figured bass on the staff.

Student's solution completed:

	I	IV	V	I	I	II	V	I
		#	#				#	
		6	7				7	

MELODIC ANALYSIS

Using the method of melodic analysis as outlined in Chapter 24, analyze the following melodies which are based on the implied harmonies of second classification, first classification, and tonic:

Het Vlooch Een Clein Wilt Voghelken   Netherlandic Folksong
    1   *Moderato*

Hertug Frydenborg Taler Til Liden Kirstin   Danish Folksong
    2   *Andantino*

Come, Sweet Lass   English Folksong
    3   *Moderato*

Aftenens Glans Mon Glode   Swedish Folksong

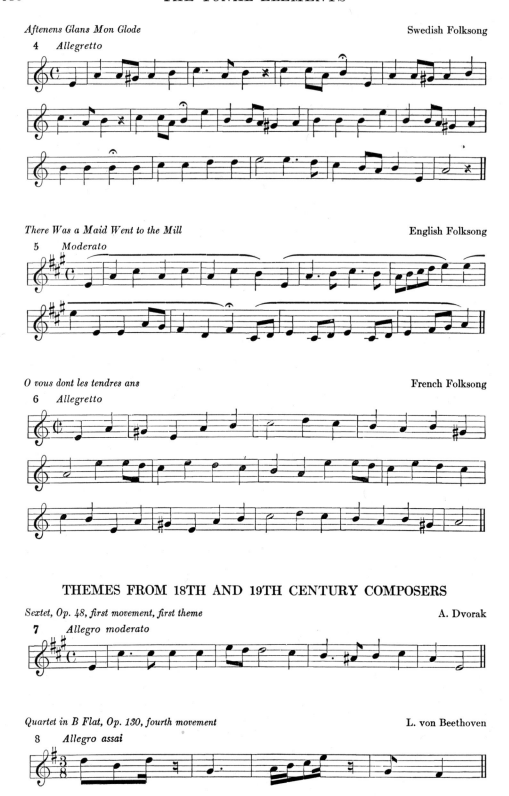

There Was a Maid Went to the Mill   English Folksong

O vous dont les tendres ans   French Folksong

THEMES FROM 18TH AND 19TH CENTURY COMPOSERS

Sextet, Op. 48, first movement, first theme   A. Dvorak

Quartet in B Flat, Op. 130, fourth movement   L. von Beethoven

Quintet in A (K 581), fourth movement — W. Mozart

Davidsbündler, Op. 6, No. 16 — R. Schumann

SIGHT-SINGING

Sight-sing the following melodies, using the same method as outlined in Chapter 24:

Mad Robin — English Folksong

The Devil's Progress — English Folksong

The Spanish Lady — English Folksong

Joan to the Maypole   English Folksong
4   Fast

To All You Ladies Now at Land   English Folksong
5   Fast

Death and the Lady   English Folksong
6   Slow

Een Aerdich Vrouken   Netherlandic Folksong
7   Moderato

Daer Spruiten Drei Boomkens in Ghenen Dal   Netherlandic Folksong
8   Moderato

THEMES FROM 18TH AND 19TH CENTURY COMPOSERS

Overture: La Muette de Portici   D. Auber
9   Allegro assai

Concerto in G, second movement J. C. Bach

10

Concerto No. 1 (3 Pianofortes and Orchestra), first movement J. S. Bach

11

Concerto No. 2 (Violin and Orchestra), first movement J. S Bach

12

Bourrée J. S. Bach

13

Overture: Le cheval de bronze D. F. Auber

14   Allegro

Gigue, from Suite No. 3 for Orchestra J. S Bach

15   Allegro

Bourrée No. 1, from English Suite No. 2 for Pianoforte J. S. Bach

16   Allegro

Minuet No. 2, from English Suite No. 4 for Pianoforte J. S. Bach

17   Moderato

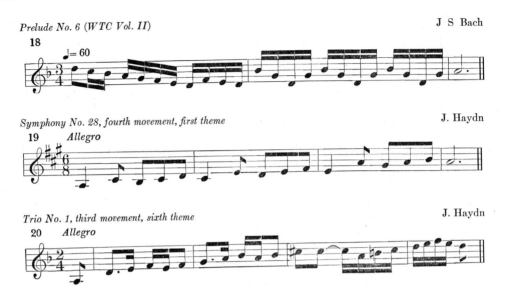

Prelude No. 6 (WTC Vol. II) — J S Bach

Symphony No. 28, fourth movement, first theme — J. Haydn

Trio No. 1, third movement, sixth theme — J. Haydn

For further sight-singing exercises, turn to the *Sight-Singing Manual*, Exercises 7, 9, 10, 11, 12, 13, 14, 19, 20, 21, 23, 24, 27, 28, 29, 30, 35, 36, 46, 48, 54, 57, and 58.

MELODIC DICTATION*

The melodic dictation exercises are based on the implied harmonic background of II, IV, V, and I. The dictation procedure will be the same as in previous chapters.

PART-WRITING

In the authentic cadence with the soprano line 8–7–8 or 3–2–1, composers may prolong the duration of the first classification harmony in the following manner:

6

In the cadence formula, the 4 sonority built on the dominant and appearing on a heavy beat is part of the dominant chord. That is, the sixth and the fourth above the bass are unessential, and they normally progress stepwise, respectively, to the

* Melodic dictation exercises will be found in the *Teachers Dictation Manual*, page 25 to 27.

fifth and third of the dominant chord. This sonority is called the *Accented Six-Four*, and it is not to be identified as a functional tonic in second inversion. The bass note of an accented six-four is doubled almost one hundred per cent of the time.

Part-write the following:

The composers' part-writing procedure for two triads in first inversion which are on consecutive tones of the scale, is as follows:

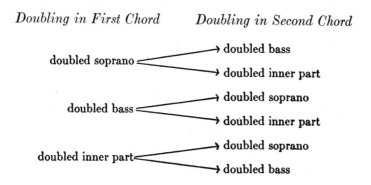

The general principle governing these progressions is: Avoid doubling an active tone. In a major key the only diatonic active tone which composers avoid doubling is the leading tone. In a minor key they avoid doubling the raised-six, raised-seven, and the natural six.*

* The natural six is frequently doubled in the VI provided the root is in the bass.

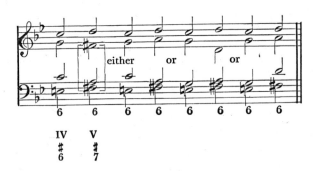

The following example begins with an incorrect doubling followed by a proper part-writing procedure.

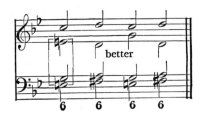

Part-write the following:

MELODIC COMPOSITION

Second classification triads are now to be included among the implied harmonies used in Chapter 24. The melodic composition procedure established in Chapter 24 will be the basis for this chapter.

EXERCISE 4. Develop into a phrase the following melodic groupings. Write at least two solutions for each melodic grouping.

EXERCISE 5. Write an original phrase based on the following tempo indications:

        1. Allegro
        2. Langsam
        3. Vivace
        4. Moderato

Give tempo rating of the unit; for example, ♩ = 92.

Vary the mode of the original phrases.

Indicate dynamics.

Devote considerable attention to developing a good manuscript.

FOUR-VOICE SETTING OF A MELODY

In selecting the chords for a melody which is in the character of a hymn, it is customary to harmonize each beat.   The selection of the chords should promote harmonic movement, as follows:

Normal progression should be used most of the time.
Repetition should be used about one-fifth as often as the normal progression.
Elision should be used sparingly.
Retrogression should be used sparingly.

Use of repetition is controlled by the rhythmic organization of a phrase.   The following example illustrates the two fundamental ways in which repetition operates in the 18th and 19th century styles:

G   I   I   V   I   IV   V   —   I

a. A chord may be repeated from a light beat to a heavy beat at the beginning
     of a feminine phrase.
b. A chord may be repeated from a heavy beat to a light beat within a phrase.
Repetition involving a light beat to a heavy beat within the phrase is not used.

With this information as a background, the harmonization of a phrase will be worked out as follows:*

1.   The phrase is feminine with a masculine ending.
2*a.* The phrase ends in a half-cadence.
2*b.* Selection of the chords
     Since the phrase is feminine, the f and a may be harmonized by the
     f-major chord.

The harmonization thus far has taken care of half of the melodic tones.

* See Chapter 24, page 164.

The b-flats imply second classification; thus, it is obvious that the normal progression from the b-flats leads to the following results:

Second classification leaves a choice of either **IV** or **II**. Although the b-flats may be harmonized with **IV** or **II**, it is probably wise to harmonize one with **IV** and the other with **II**.

The roots of the chords placed on the staff appear as follows:

A performance of the harmonization of a melody using the fundamental bass is rarely aurally satisfactory, even though the chord progressions in themselves are correct. For this reason, it is important to realize that the bass which one hears in the course of a composition represents roots as well as thirds, occasional fifths, and sevenths of chords.

The hymn and chorale style of the 18th and 19th century uses a bass-counterpoint.* For the present, the bass counterpoint will contain roots and thirds of chords. The interval relationship with the soprano will be octaves, perfect fifths, thirds, and sixths. The fundamental bass of the example below, converted into a bass-counterpoint, will be as follows:

* Counterpoint is the art of combining two or more voices, emphasizing in each the principles of melodic composition.

THE BASS COUNTERPOINT

The bass and soprano help to bind together a musical composition just as the outside covers of a book help to keep the contents intact. The bass counterpoint moves in four ways in relation to the soprano: stationary, oblique, similar, and contrary motion. Let us analyze the following chorale phrases and tabulate the motion of the bass counterpoint to the soprano:

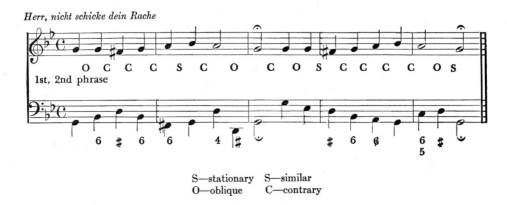

Herr, nicht schicke dein Rache

O   C   C   C   S   C   O   C   O   S   C   C   C   C   O   S

1st, 2nd phrase

S—stationary   S—similar
O—oblique   C—contrary

Taking the oblique movement instances in the order of their occurrence, the intervallic relationships between bass and soprano are as follows:

1. Octave—sixth
2. Fifth—fifth (caused by leap of an octave; frequent in the cadence formula)
3. Octave—third
4. Sixth—fifth

Taking the similar movement instances in the order of occurrence, the intervallic relationships between bass and soprano are as follows:

1. Third—third
2. Third—third
3. Fifth—octave (bass notes being roots of chords)

Taking the contrary movement instances in the order of their occurrence, the intervallic relationships between bass and soprano are as follows:

1. Sixth—third
2. Third—sixth
3. Sixth—third
4. Third—fifth
5. Fifth—octave

6. Third—sixth
7. Sixth—octave
8. Octave—third (tenth)
9. Third—sixth

The following chorales illustrate the stationary bass and soprano:

At 1, the stationary bass and soprano occur on the heavy beat and light beat.

At 2, the stationary bass and soprano occur at the opening of a feminine phrase. The stationary device is rare. It is usually encountered at the beginning of a phrase, and it is occasionally found in a feminine cadence. It is extremely rare within the phrase from a heavy beat to a light beat.

The following table, based on an analysis of many chorales of Bach, Handel, Graun, Mendelssohn, and others, illustrates the frequency of the four ways in which the bass and soprano lines travel simultaneously:

> Contrary.......... 46%
> Similar............. 30%
> Oblique........... 23%
> Stationary......... 1%

Almost any combination of intervals is possible between the bass and soprano lines when they move in contrary motion. The only set of intervals which Bach and the others avoid in chorale style is the octave to octave or the fifth to fifth.

At 1, these octaves are called *octaves by contrary motion*.

At 2, these fifths are called *fifths by contrary motion*.

Oblique motion provides many combinations of intervals. Due to the fact that one voice remains stationary while the other moves either toward or away from it, parallel fifths and octaves, which are out of the style, cannot occur between the bass and soprano.

Similar motion existing between the bass and soprano, however, presents some problems which must be thoroughly mastered. The following table shows the common intervals which follow each other in the similar motion of the bass and soprano:

Octave—fifth }	Usually one voice moves by step.
Fifth—octave }	The bass notes are roots of chords.
Third—third }	Most frequent
Sixth—sixth }	

In similar motion a sixth to a fifth and a third to a fifth, forbidden by theorists, are occasionally found in the chorales; for instance:

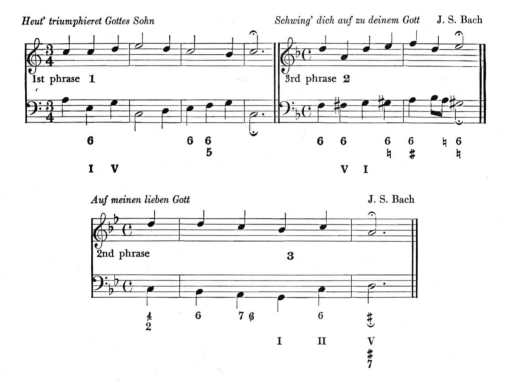

At 1, the sixth in similar motion to a fifth appears in the progression of the first inversion of the I to V.

At 2, a third in similar motion to a fifth appears in the progression of the first inversion of the V to I.

At 3, a third in similar motion to an octave appears in the progression of the I to the first inversion of II with the third in the soprano.

The movement to the fifth at 1 and 2 is called *hidden fifths;* the movement to the octave at 3 is called *hidden octaves.* Bach does not often indulge in hidden fifths and octaves between the bass and soprano in similar motion. It is interesting to note that whenever Bach uses hidden fifths and octaves, he consistently uses the tonic chord as one of the chords in the progression. The illustration at 1 is the most frequent of these rare examples of hidden fifths and octaves.*

The bass has many characteristics common to good melody writing.

In the bass counterpoint, certain melodic intervals are avoided. This is true, for the most part, in the instrumental styles as well as in the vocal style. The intervals avoided are the augmented second, the augmented fourth, and the major seventh. The minor seventh and the diminished seventh are extremely rare. Leaps of the major and minor sixth and the octave are infrequent. Leaps of the perfect fifth, perfect fourth, major and minor third, and stepwise motion of major and minor seconds are the most common intervals.

One of the most important factors in melody writing is concerned with contour. Although the bass melody is sometimes forced to give up good contour for harmonic reasons, the underlying qualifications of good melody writing prevail.

Three directions of the melodic movement are possible from a given point; it may ascend, descend, or remain stationary. The melody should never be allowed to continue stepwise in the same direction for more than five or six notes of different pitch. Observe the contour in the following bass melodies:

The bass counterpoint should reverse direction after a wide leap, as illustrated in the following examples:

If it is at all possible, every bass counterpoint should have in its contour a high note and a low note which are not repeated. *The high note is sometimes called the climax note; the low note is called the anticlimax note.* It is not always possible to write a bass counterpoint which will contain both notes. An investigation of many

---

* The student may use hidden fifths and octaves occasionally. If, however, he abuses the privilege, the instructor should immediately consider them errors, in light of the fact that the device is used sparingly.

counterpoints reveals that if they contain only one, the climax tone is favored.   In the following examples, the highest and lowest notes for the entire phrase appear only once:

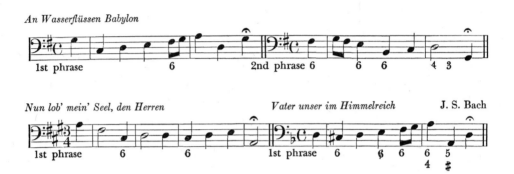

An Wasserflüssen Babylon

1st phrase   6   2nd phrase 6   6 6   4 3

Nun lob' mein' Seel, den Herren   *Vater unser im Himmelreich*   J. S. Bach

1st phrase   6   6   1st phrase   6   6 6   6 5

Applying this discussion and analysis, observe and study how the chorale melody of the example below can be given further harmonizations for each of which three bass counterpoints are written.

In the chorale or hymn-tune style it is important to realize that the best four-voice setting depends upon good harmonic treatment and a good bass counterpoint. It is well for the student to recognize that there are many harmonizations possible for any given melody. These harmonizations may be correct, but from an artistic sense they may vary from artistic beauty to pure academic dullness. At first the student lacks the sense of evaluating what sounds well. To develop this judgment the student should create as many correct harmonizations as possible so that he may be able to select for himself what he likes best out of *what he creates.*

EXERCISE 6. Harmonize each chorale phrase at least three different ways. Compose three bass counterpoints to each of the harmonizations. Each bass counterpoint is to be figured. Supply the chord functions.

The chorale melody with its figured-bass counterpoint has the appearance of the part-writing and keyboard exercises to which were added the alto and tenor. As soon as the student shows consistent ability in selecting the chords and writing the figured-bass counterpoint in these exercises, he may proceed to treat them like the part-writing and keyboard exercises given previously, and complete them by adding alto and tenor.

EXERCISE 7. Make at least two four-voice settings of any of the chorale melodies of Exercise 6.

Chapter 26

The Major-Minor Seventh Chord;
The Dominant Seventh

In accord with the conventional 18th and 19th century chordal construction, a *seventh chord* is formed by adding a third above the fifth of any type triad. The interval of the third above the fifth may be major or minor. The identification of the type seventh chord depends upon two factors: first, the tonal construction of the triad; and, second, the interval produced by the root and seventh. The name of the FACE♭ seventh chord is determined in the following manner:

First factor	FAC	major triad
Second factor	F—E♭	minor seventh

FACE♭ is called a *major-minor seventh chord*. The abbreviation for a major-minor seventh chord is Mm⁷.

Seventh chords appear through the linear movement of the voices of 15th and 16th century compositions of three or more voices; a limited number of functional

Vorspiel zu: Dies sind die heilgen zehn Gebot   J. C. Bach

seventh chords is used during the 17th century.* In the third measure of the

---

* See Chapter 15 of A. I. McHose, *Contrapuntal Harmonic Technique of the 18th Century* (New York, Appleton-Century-Crofts, 1947).

197

this example, the alto d progresses downwards to the dissonant c, the seventh, which in turn prepares the suspension note c in the last measure. The suspension is given an ornamental resolution. The third and fourth beats contain the d-f#-a-c-seventh chord which has dominant function. This example illustrates the stepwise introduction of the seventh of a seventh chord. The seventh chord is found on a heavy pulsation within a quadruple measure.

Non-harmonic tones often produce groupings of notes that are apparently seventh chords. The question of whether such groupings of notes are legitimate seventh chords or not can only be determined by the tempo and rhythmic context in each case. The next example shows at (1) and (2) how two descending melodic lines form a seventh chord spelling on a light pulsation. They cannot be called seventh chords because the note d in the bass and the note d in the tenor are passing tones in the e-major triad background.

When a seventh chord is identified, its seventh appropriates the rights and privileges which the root, third, and fifth possess in major or minor triads. The seventh is now an essential tone, and it can prepare a suspension, introduce an anticipation, etc. Since it is a dissonance, its introduction and resolution are carefully governed by rules derived from the practices of the composers. The 18th and 19th century composers introduce and resolve the seventh as a part of the following melodic figures:

Character of Melodic Figure	Name	Use in the Progression Containing the Major-Minor Seventh Chord
	Suspension figure	

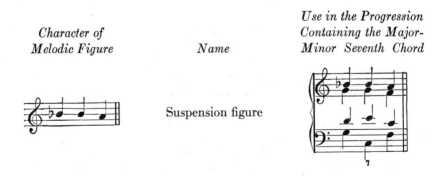

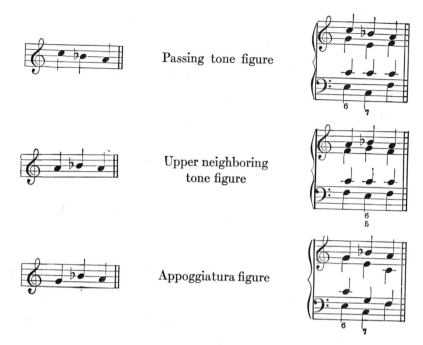

Passing tone figure

Upper neighboring tone figure

Appoggiatura figure

The major-minor seventh chord came into use during the 17th century, and it is found as the most popular type of seventh chord in the music of the 18th and 19th centuries. During these centuries, it is one of the important chords in the first classification, its roots being on the dominant. However, the major-minor seventh chord appears in other classifications as an altered chord. For this reason, the author urges one to guard against the familiar and thoughtless nickname which is used, namely, dominant seventh type or five-seven type.

The important aural properties of the major-minor seventh chord are the basic major triad, tritone, and minor seventh.

To spell any major-minor seventh chord from any given root, spell the basic major triad, spell a diminished triad using the third of the major triad as the root, then recite the spelling in the order of the root, third, fifth, and seventh. For example, spell the e-flat major-minor seventh chord. The e-flat major triad is e♭gb♭; the diminished triad spelling on g is gb♭d♭; the e-flat major-minor seventh chord spelling is e♭gb♭d♭.

EXERCISE 1. Be able to spell any major-minor seventh chord.
EXERCISE 2. Place the major-minor seventh chord on the staff, considering each given tone as the root.

EXERCISE 3. Play the major-minor seventh chord, considering each given tone as the root.

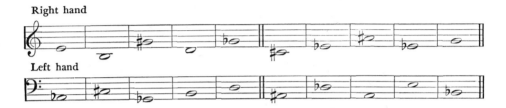

PLAYING THE MAJOR-MINOR SEVENTH CHORD

EXERCISE 4. Play any major-minor seventh in the position of the octave, third, fifth, or seventh.

Instructions: Cover the given chord with the left hand. The right hand then arranges the chord spelling desired. The chord is to be played in four voices. Do not double the root when the third, fifth, or seventh is in the soprano. When the octave is in the soprano, omit the fifth.

Example: Play the f-sharp major-minor seventh in the position of the third.

The major-minor seventh chord has three inversions.

Bass Tone	Name of Inversion
Third..............	First inversion
Fifth..............	Second inversion
Seventh............	Third inversion

In the inversions, the major-minor seventh must have all chord members present; in four-voice texture no chord member is doubled. For example, the third inversion of a seventh chord in the position of the seventh or the second inversion of the chord in the position of the fifth are not used in four-voice writing.

EXERCISE 5. Play a major-minor seventh in any inversion.

Example: Play the third inversion of the e-major-minor seventh in the position of the third.

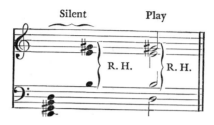

The major-minor seventh chord appears in the first inversion as a dominant seventh. In a major key its symbol is V⁷; in a minor key its symbol is V⁷.

The figured bass symbols for a seventh chord and its inversions are as follows:

Figurations for the seventh chord's root in the bass may be:

$$7, 7, 7, 7$$
$$\natural \quad \sharp \quad 5$$
$$\sharp$$

Figurations for the first inversion may be:

$$6, 6, 6$$
$$5 \quad 5 \quad 5$$
$$\sharp \quad 3$$

Figurations for the second inversion may be:

$$6, \ 6, \ 6$$
$$4 \quad 4 \quad 4 \quad 4$$
$$3 \quad 3 \ \flat \ 3$$

6
4 or 4   6   4
3   3   4 or ♭
          ♭

6
4
3

6
4 or 4
3   3

Figurations for the third inversion may be:

$$4, \ 4, \ 2, \ 6$$
$$2 \quad 2 \qquad 4$$
$$2$$

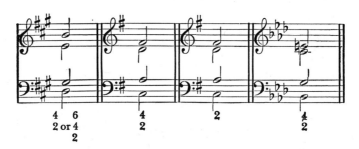

4   6   4   2   4
2 or 4   2   2
2

The basic voice leading in the progression V⁷–I is best illustrated by the use of five-voice writing:

F♯ minor

V⁷   I
♯
7

The deductions which are made from this basic progression are as follows:

1. If the root is in an upper part, it is kept as the common tone.
2. The third rises to the root of the tonic. In four-voice writing this is true when the third is in either the soprano or the bass.
3. The fifth descends to the root of the tonic. When the fifth is in the bass in four-voice writing, it sometimes rises to the third of the tonic.

4. The seventh descends to the third of the tonic triad. The seventh, either in the soprano or an inner voice, may rise to the fifth of the tonic triad under one condition, namely, in the progression of the second inversion of the dominant seventh to the first inversion of the tonic triad. The seventh in the soprano may also be given an ornamental resolution. Under these conditions, it may be left by leap or ascending step, but it invariably resolves in this ornamentation to the third of the tonic triad.

Compare the deductions with the typical composer's progressions of V^7–I:

At (a), (c), and (d) the upper voices adhere to voice leading established in the basic chord progression of five voices. However, at (a) and (c) the tonic triad is incomplete. To obtain a complete tonic one must break the tendencies of the basic progression. At (b) the third of the V^7 descends by leap to the fifth of the tonic. At (d), by using an incomplete V^7, one can obtain a complete tonic and at the same time use the basic voice leading. All four progressions are good. Bach prefers (b) and (d); Handel prefers (a) and (c). It is these little preferences, when added together, which define the stylistic differences between contemporary composers.

The inversions of the dominant seventh chord have all chord members present. One rarely encounters an incomplete inverted seventh chord. In the following examples note that the basic voice leading is carried out in most instances.

The tendencies of the basic voice leading are carried out at 1, 2, 3, 4, 5, 7, and 10. At 6, the seventh c rises to the fifth of the tonic triad. This particular irregularity is confined to the progression of the second inversion of the V⁷ to the first inversion of the I. The progression was established during the 18th century, and it was used sparingly by Bach, Handel, and their contemporaries. At 8, 9, and 12, the two least active tones, the root and fifth, leap to tones of the tonic triad in order to have the preferred doubling in the first inversion of the tonic, namely, the doubled soprano.

EXERCISE 6. Complete at the keyboard the following progressions V⁷–I.

EXERCISE 7. Play any position of a dominant seventh chord, and resolve it to either a major tonic or a minor tonic.

Example: Play the first inversion of the b-dominant seventh chord in the position of the seventh, and resolve it in the key of e-minor.

THE APPLICATION OF THE THEORY OF INVERSION

Exercise 8.* Be able to recognize the root of a major-minor seventh chord.

    Example: A series of major-minor seventh chords will be played. Listen to the seventh chord and sing the root, using a neutral syllable. (Same procedure as Exercise 7 of Chapter 15.)

Exercise 9.* Identify the root, third, fifth, or seventh in the soprano of a major-minor seventh chord.

    Example: A series of major-minor seventh chords will be played. Listen to the soprano and determine whether it is the root, third, fifth or seventh. (Same procedure as Exercise 8 of Chapter 15.)

    Note: This exercise may be practised with the student giving first oral and then written response. When writing, use

        1 for the root
        3 for the third
        5 for the fifth
        7 for the seventh

EXERCISE 10. Identify the root, third, fifth, and seventh in the bass of a major-minor seventh chord.

    Example: A series of major-minor seventh chords will be played. Listen to the bass and determine whether it is the root, third, fifth, or seventh. (Same procedure as Exercise 9 of Chapter 15.)

Oral and written response should be performed in two ways:

1. Identifying the chord member by using 1, 3, 5, and 7
2. Naming the inversion as follows:

    root in bass   not inverted
    third in bass   first inversion
    fifth in bass   second inversion
    seventh in bass third inversion

EXERCISE 11. Identify the root, third, fifth, and seventh in the bass and soprano of a major-minor seventh chord. (Same procedure as Exercise 11 of Chapter 15.)

    This exercise should be practised by having the student's response either oral or written. In both oral and written response, emphasize terminology. For example, the terminology response to the chord played below is "the third inversion of a major-minor seventh chord in the position of the third."

EXERCISE 12. Writing the major-minor seventh chord on staff paper from dictation when the soprano tone is given.

Example: The instructor names f in the soprano and plays the third inversion of the f-major-minor seventh chord in the position of the octave. The student's solution appears as follows:

Performing this exercise for a series of chords, on the blackboard copy the soprano tones which are to be used in the following manner:

EXERCISE 13. Describing a chord from dictation when the soprano tone is known. (Same procedure as Exercise 13 of Chapter 15.)

INTERVALS AND THE MAJOR-MINOR SEVENTH CHORD

The major-minor seventh chord introduces two new intervals. 1 up to 7 is a minor seventh, and 7 up to 1 is a major second.

Assignment. Make a complete table, showing the intervals which can imply a major-minor seventh chord.

The exercises for developing the intervals in the major-minor seventh chord correspond in the same order to the previous interval drills. If there is any doubt concerning the procedure, refer to Chapter 16.

EXERCISE 14. Playing intervallic relationships based on the major-minor seventh chord.

EXERCISE 15. Singing any intervallic relationship based on the major-minor seventh chord.

EXERCISE 16. Recognizing the intervallic relationship from a given pitch based on a major-minor seventh chord.

EXERCISE 17. Intervals based on the major-minor seventh chord placed on the staff from dictation.

EXERCISE 18. Recognizing from dictation and placing the interval on the staff and naming the interval. The following intervals are to be dictated: major second, minor second, major third, minor third, perfect fourth, augmented fourth, perfect fifth, diminished fifth, major sixth, minor sixth, minor seventh, and perfect octave. (Same procedure as in Exercise 17 of Chapter 21.) Example:

As a Melodic Interval

Per. 5th   M 6th   M 2nd   m 7th   Aug. 4th

As a Harmonic Interval

Per. 5th   m 3rd   dim. 5th   m 7th   m 6th

HARMONIC DICTATION

The harmonic dictation drills leading to a musical understanding of the dominant seventh chord are given below. Each drill is to be given in the order of presentation. Do not progress to the next drill exercise until each drill is mastered.

EXERCISE 19. Harmonic dictation drills leading to the identification of the dominant seventh chord in a major or minor key.
A phrase is played.
1. Sing the root of each chord.
2. Recite or write the type of each chord.
3. Recite or write the classification of each chord.
4. Recite the name of each chord or write the symbols.
5. Using staff paper, write the soprano, figured bass, and the symbols.

MELODIC ANALYSIS AND SIGHT-SINGING

From the standpoint of aesthetic musical values, it is advisable that the student realize that the dominant seventh chord can be overemphasized in musical texture. Some students, once they master the dominant seventh chord, seem to feel that the use of a dominant triad indicates naïveté. This is gross misunderstanding of how the elements of music are combined to form a composition. This idea should be constantly applied from now on in our study.

As we have seen, there are two points of view for melodic analysis. In sight-singing the harmonic implications of a melody are simple and direct in their meaning. There is a resistance to too much harmonic change. On the other hand, a harmonization of a melody, leading to an artistic setting, begins with a simple harmonic analysis which is quite similar to the one used for sight-singing. From this basic harmonic background an artistic setting can be synthesized.

For sight-singing purposes, a melody can at times imply relatively few harmonies through the use of the dominant seventh chord.

The linking together of the two a's and the c in the second measure implies a d-major-minor seventh chord which is more fundamental than the a-minor triad. In the last measure there is nothing to indicate an implied seventh chord; yet measures two and four have the same fundamental.

EXERCISE 20. Melodic analysis.
    Analyze the given melodies by identifying the basic implied harmonies and non-harmonic tones.

FOLKSONGS

FUGUE SUBJECTS

J. S. Bach

G. Handel

P. Fafaro

G. Handel

THEMES FROM 18TH AND 19TH CENTURY COMPOSERS

Sonata in G (K 189)

W. Mozart

Part of "Minuet" from String Quintette in A Major

L. Boccherini

Part of Theme from Sonata, Op. 78

L. von Beethoven

Trois Fantaisies on Caprices:
First Fantasy, theme transposed (incomplete)   F. Mendelssohn

10   *Andante con moto*

EXERCISE 21. Sight-singing melodies which contain the implied dominant seventh chord.

FOLKSONGS

1 *"La Marmotte en vie"*   French
   Grazioso

2 *"Dans les Gardes Françaises"*   French
   Lively

3 *Christmas Song*   French
   Dolce

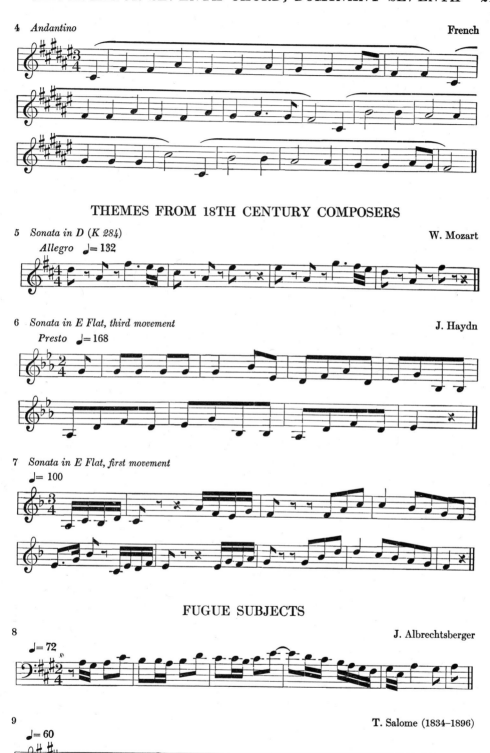

THEMES FROM 18TH CENTURY COMPOSERS

5 *Sonata in D (K 284)*   W. Mozart

6 *Sonata in E Flat, third movement*   J. Haydn

7 *Sonata in E Flat, first movement*

FUGUE SUBJECTS

8   J. Albrechtsberger

9   T. Salome (1834–1896)

The exercises which imply the dominant seventh chord found in the *Sight-Singing Manual* are as follows: 19, 28, 32, 36, 38, 39, 40, 41, 42, 46, 48, 52, 53, 55, 65, 66, 67, 73, 75, 113, 115, 134, 135, 138, and 140.

MELODIC DICTATION*

EXERCISE 22. Melodic dictation.

The dictation procedure is the same as in former chapters. The melodies will contain the implied harmonic background of I, V, V⁷, IV, and II.

PART-WRITING

ROOT POSITION OF THE DOMINANT SEVENTH

When the 7th of the V⁷ is prepared by the suspension figure, the V is preceded by chords of the second classification, namely, II and IV.

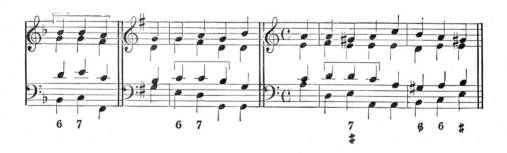

When the 7th of the V⁷ is prepared by the passing tone figure, the V is introduced by either tonic and its inversions or by the V triad in root position or first inversion, but not by chords of the second classification.

* Melodic dictation exercises are found in the *Teachers Dictation Manual*, Part II, #55 through #68.

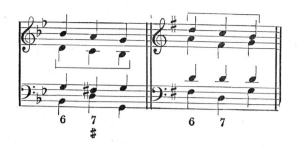

When the 7th of the V⁷ is prepared by the appoggiatura figure, it is usually preceded by the V triad or its first inversion and rarely by chords in the second classification.

Since the preparation of the 7th of the V⁷ by use of the neighboring tone figure is infrequent, this study will be omitted for the present.

General deductions from the foregoing discussion and examples are summarized as follows:

1. All the figures explained on pages 198 and 199, with the exception of the neighboring tone figure, are used in connection with the part-writing of the V⁷.
2. The seventh in accord with the design of the preparation figure must descend.
3. The seventh may be used in the soprano, alto, or tenor.

EXERCISE 23. Part-writing the root position of the V⁷.

THE INVERSIONS OF THE DOMINANT SEVENTH

When the 7th of the first inversion of the V^7 is prepared by the suspension figure, the V^7 is preceded by chords of the second classification.

When the 7th of the first inversion of the V^7 is prepared by the passing tone figure, the V^7 is preceded by the first inversion of the I, or by the V triad in root position.

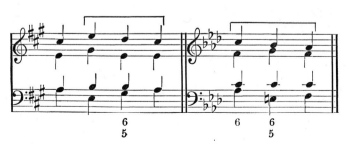

When the 7th of the first inversion of the V⁷ is prepared by the neighboring tone figure, the V⁷ is preceded by the root position of the I.

When the 7th of the first inversion of the V⁷ is prepared by the appoggiatura figure, the V⁷ is preceded by either the first inversion of the I or by the first inversion of the V triad.

In four-voice writing the second inversion of the V⁷ is rare. In addition, the seventh of the second inversion of the V⁷ is usually limited to one preparation, the passing tone figure. The passing tone figure may descend or ascend. In the ascending passing tone figure, the 7th of the chord resolves unconventionally up to the 5th of the I. (See deduction 4, on page 203.)

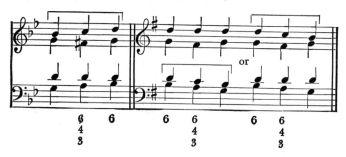

When the 7th of the third inversion of the V⁷ is prepared by the suspension figure, the V⁷ is introduced by the IV or the first inversion of II.

When the 7th of the third inversion of the V⁷ is prepared by the passing tone figure, the V⁷ is introduced by the root position of the V triad.

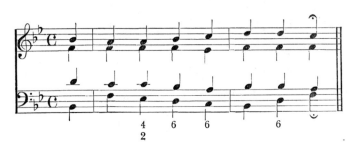

When the 7th of the third inversion of the V⁷ is prepared by the neighboring tone figure, the V⁷ is introduced by the first inversion of the I.

When the 7th of the third inversion of the V⁷ is prepared by the appoggiatura figure, the V⁷ is introduced by either the V triad or the first inversion of the V triad or the I.

EXERCISE 24. Part-writing the inversions of the V⁷.

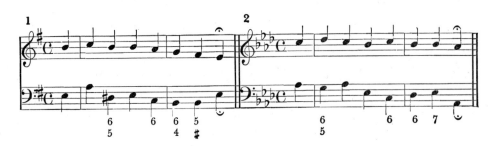

J. S. Bach

MELODIC COMPOSITION

The implication of the dominant seventh contributes much to melodic composition.

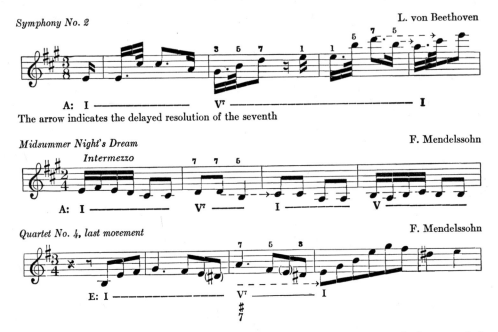

The arrow indicates the delayed resolution of the seventh

Analyze the method of approach and resolution of the seventh (contour) in at least fifteen melodies used for melodic analysis and sight-singing in this chapter.

EXERCISE 25. Develop into a period the following figures:
End the first phrase with a half-cadence.

EXERCISE 26. Compose original period melodies, using the following tempo directions:

1. Moderato $-\dfrac{6}{8}$ —minor key

2. Adagio $\quad-\dfrac{4}{4}$ —major key

3. Grave $\quad-\dfrac{3}{2}$ —minor key

4. Andantino $-\dfrac{2}{4}$ —major key

FOUR-VOICE SETTING OF A MELODY

The dominant seventh chord introduces the minor seventh, diminished fifth, augmented fourth, and major second when the bass counterpoint is composed to the melody. Examine the following examples which illustrate the use of these intervals:

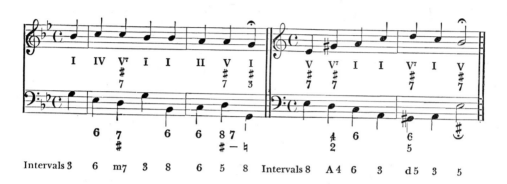

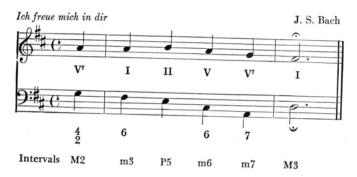

Ich freue mich in dir   J. S. Bach

EXERCISE 27. Use the following assignments for the given melodies:

    Drill 1. Make at least two harmonizations.

           To each harmonization write three figured bass counterpoints.

    Drill 2. Compose and part-write at least two settings.

EXERCISE 28. Compose in chorale style an original phrase using the chords studied thus
far.

1. $\frac{3}{4}$ meter in a minor key.

2. $\frac{4}{4}$ meter in a major key.

Chapter 27

The Triad in the Third Classification: Submediant

The diatonic triad which is found in the third classification of a major or a minor key is as follows:

The Triad in the Third Classification

Major Key

Name	Symbol	Type Chord
Submediant	VI	Minor Triad

Minor Key

Name	Symbol	Type Chord
Submediant	VI	Major Triad

The following examples illustrate the use of the submediant triad in a variety of musical textural styles during the 18th and 19th centuries:

Overture: Cosi fan tutte — W. Mozart — Andante

Es ist gewisslich an der Zeit   J. S. Bach

G: I   VI ―――――――― II⁷ V⁷ I   II⁷ ― V   I

Wir Christenleut'   J. S. Bach

F♯: I ―――――――― V ― VI   IV   V ――――――― I
                  ♯   ♯
                  7   7

Sonata, Op. 120, second movement   F. Schubert
     Andante

D: I ―――――――――― V⁷ ――――――― VI   V⁷   I

Sonata, Op. 53   L. von Beethoven

F: IV   IV   V ― V⁷ : VI ― II   V⁷   I
    ♯   ♯ ♭
    4   4 6

PART-WRITING AND KEYBOARD; NORMAL PROGRESSION AND DECEPTIVE CADENCE

The submediant triad progresses to the chords of the second classification. The fundamental bass movement will be either down a fifth or a third. In a major key, VI to II or the first inversion of II is a frequent normal progression. The composers, however, in a minor key avoid the progression from VI to II and prefer the progression from VI to the first inversion of II.

At (*a*) and (*c*) the soprano line uses the scale steps 1–2–7–1 and 3–4–2–1. Each chord has two roots, a third, and a fifth. When VI progresses to II, the part-writing principle using the common tone is used. At (*b*) and (*d*) the bass is doubled in the II. The doubled third is approached and left by contrary motion. At (*b*) above the first inversion of the II could have the soprano tone doubled in the tenor.

Part-write the following:

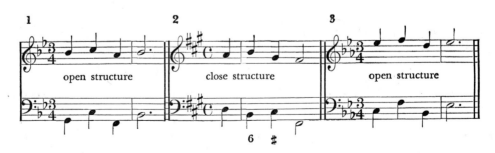

Play at the keyboard the following:

EXERCISE 1. Be able to play in any major key VI–II–V–I and in any major or minor key VI–II₆–V–I in the various ways outlined in the previous drills.

The normal progression from VI to IV requires a new principle of part-writing. When one triad progresses to another which has its root a third below the first,

keep the common tones in the same voices, and move the remaining voice step-wise
to the next triad tone.*

Example:

Part-write the following:

* This method of part-writing is likewise applicable if the root of the second chord is a third above that of the
first chord.

Play at the keyboard the following:

EXERCISE 2. Be able to play in any major or minor key VI–IV–V–I in the various ways
outlined in the previous drills.

A *Deceptive Cadence* is established by substituting either the first inversion of
the tonic triad, tonic discord, or another chord for the octave position of the tonic
chord.*   In most instances, the deceptive cadence contains a retrogression.   The
earliest deceptive cadences found in the period of the 18th and 19th century composition use the following progressions: V–VI

$$V–VI \text{ (rarely used in the 18th century)}$$
$$\flat\flat$$
$$36$$

The following settings of a chorale melody illustrate these deceptive cadences:

O Gott, du frommer Gott   *Vater unser im Himmelreich*   J. S. Bach

*This is a broad definition which includes Wagner's use of the deceptive cadence.

A very infrequent 18th century deceptive cadence which foreshadows the
manner in which the 19th century composers expanded the harmonic possibilities
of this cadence is as follows:

Lobt Gott, ihr Christen, allzugleich   J. S. Bach

Composers using the deceptive cadence V–VI invariably double the third in
the submediant triad.   From this cadence a second part-writing method for handling the foreign progression is made possible.

When one triad progresses to another which has its root a second above the
first, move the third of the first triad in thirds or tenths with the bass, and
move the remaining upper voices to the nearest tones of the next chord in
contrary motion to the bass.

The second triad in this progression will have one root, two thirds, and one fifth.

Part-write the following deceptive cadences:

Play at the keyboard the following deceptive cadences:

EXERCISE 3. Be able to play a deceptive cadence in any major or minor key, using the soprano lines outlined in the previous drills.

HARMONIC DICTATION*

Characteristics:

    a. The triad in the third classification progresses normally to chords of the second classification.

    b. Its root is on the submediant. (See Chapter 22, p. 131.)

The harmonic dictation drills will be on the same order as those practised in Chapter 24.

Drill: A phrase will be played twice. As it is repeated, sing the root of the chord.

Drill: A phrase will be played twice. As it is repeated, identify orally or in writing the type of each chord.

Drill: While you are singing the root of each chord in an exercise, the instructor may halt the phrase at any point. Sing the root of the chord to which you believe the last chord should progress.

* The exercises for this section are found in the *Teachers Dictation Manual,* pages 66 through 73.

Note: If the root of the chord at the point at which the phrase was halted wants to progress to the root of a chord in the second classification, the chord belongs to the third classification.

Example:

Instructor plays:

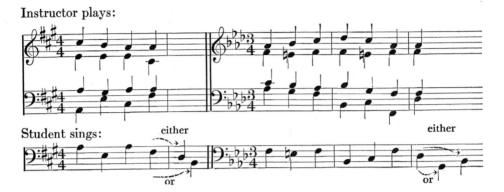

Student sings:

The previous drill establishes the normal progression for the chord of the third classification. A chord which has its root on the submediant normally progresses to chords in the second classification. A tonic chord, usually in first inversion, may interrupt the normal progression of a third-classification chord to a second-classification chord.

Drill: As a phrase is played at least three times, recite or write the classification of each chord.

I—Tonic

1st Cl.—First Classification

2nd Cl.—Second Classification

3rd Cl.—Third Classification

Drill: As a phrase is played at least three times, recite or write the name of each chord.

THE ELISION AND RETROGRESSION OF THE TRIAD IN THE THIRD CLASSIFICATION

The elision VI to V is quite frequent. Occasionally the tonic triad appears between the elision VI to V. The retrogression V to VI appears within the phrase and in the deceptive cadence. The retrogression VII to VI is infrequent and occurs only in a major key.

The dictation drills will be in the same order as those practised in Chapter 25.

Drill: A phrase will be played twice. As it is repeated, recite or write the character of the harmonic movement.

Drill: As a phrase is played at least three times, recite or write the name of each chord.

Drill: As the instructor gives the key, write the chord symbols, soprano, and figured bass on the staff.

PART-WRITING

A summary of part-writing procedures is as follows:

1. The triad containing its root in the bass
   a. Roots a fifth apart
      (1) Keep the common tone; the remaining voices move by step to the next chord tones.
      (2) The three upper voices move in similar motion to the next chord tones.
   b. Roots a second apart
      (1) The three upper voices move in contrary motion to the bass.
      (2) If the second chord is a scale step above the root of the first triad, move stepwise in similar motion the voice a third above or tenth above the bass, and the remaining voices move contrary to the bass. This method of voice leading is good for the progressions I–II and V–VI, and it is not to be used for IV–V. The composers avoid doubling the third in the dominant chord because it is the leading tone.
   c. Roots a third apart
      (1) Keep the two common tones, and move the remaining voice stepwise. The root of the second triad may be either a third above or a third below the first.
2. Triad with the doubled third
      A triad with the doubled third may progress to another which has its root, above or below, a fifth, second, or third. Try to leave the doubled third by either contrary or oblique motion, and lastly by similar motion.*
3. Triad in first inversion
      The part-writing leading to and from a triad in first inversion is controlled by the doubled chord member in the chord in first inversion.** Approach to and departure from the doubled chord member should follow the general frequency usage by the composers. They prefer contrary and oblique motion to similar motion.

Part-write the following:

* See *Contrapuntal Harmonic Technique*, by A. I. McHose, pages 62 and 63.
** See Chapter 25, page 172.

Thus far, the most frequently used part-writing principles have been presented. There are, however, a number of principles which the composers use sparingly. These methods of part-writing should be considered as conventional exceptions, because they stem from conventional procedures.

When one triad progresses to another which has its root a fifth above or below the first triad, keep the common tone in the same voice, move the third of the first triad to the third of the second, and move the remaining voice by step to the next triad tone.*

Weg, mein Herz, mit den Gedanken

* See *Contrapuntal Harmonic Technique*, McHose, Chapter 5.

O Haupt voll Blut und Wunden — J. S. Bach

At (*a*) and (*b*), the third of the first triad leaps a perfect fourth to the third of the second triad. In a minor key the leap of a diminished fourth is acceptable, especially in the authentic cadence. At (*c*), the third of the first triad leaps a perfect fourth to the third of the second triad. This method of voice leading is practically limited to V–I, I–V, I–IV, and IV–I. This leap of the third of one triad to the third of another can be used only in the tenor or soprano voices. The leap of a fifth is used, but it is most infrequent.

When a triad in the position of the fifth progresses down a fifth to the octave position of a triad with a tripled root, the third and fifth of the first move diatonically to the root of the second triad, and the root of the first triad descends a third to the third of the second triad.*

Von Gott will ich nicht lassen — J. S. Bach   *O Traurigkeit* — G. F. Handel

At (*a*) and (*b*), the triad with the tripled root appears as the last chord in the perfect authentic cadence. A triad with a tripled root rarely appears within a phrase. When it is found, the functions are either tonic or dominant. At (*a*), Bach prefers to use a passing seventh when he uses a tonic with a tripled root.

---

* See *Contrapuntal Harmonic Technique*, by A. I. McHose, Chapter 5, pages 50 and 51.

Part-write the following:

THE FOUR-VOICE SETTING OF THE MELODY

EXERCISE 4. Use the following drills for the given melodies:

    Drill 1. Make at least two harmonizations.

            To each harmonization write three figured bass counterpoints.

Drill 2. Compose and part-write at least two settings.

EXERCISE 5. To the settings of 1, 4, 6, and 8 add an original consequent phrase which ends in a perfect authentic cadence. The form will be a period.

Chapter 28

The Augmented Triad

❧

The augmented triad appears in the pre-18th century music as a structure composed of a major third and a minor sixth erected upon the same bass tone.

In the following examples, observe how the early composers approach and leave this sonority by step-wise motion:

Dolorosi martir   L. Marenzio

The structure arranged in the order of thirds is composed of two major thirds.

The aural effect of this sonority does not identify the two major thirds. The musical mind analyzes the sonority according to the following procedure:

The interval at (*a*) is a major third. At (*b*) the interval which is composed of eight tempered half-tones is called an augmented fifth. The chord is, then, a major

augmented fifth sonority, namely, a major third enveloped by an augmented fifth. The inversion of the augmented fifth is a diminished fourth. The diminished fourth is composed of four half-tones. It may be readily observed that the augmented triad divides the tempered octave into three equal intervals.

Four half-tones
Four half-tones
Four half-tones

For this reason, it is impossible to determine the root of an isolated augmented triad. For example, the same sound can be spelled enharmonically as follows:

roots

An augmented triad's root can be identified only through the musical context.

Not all notated augmented triads are analyzed as such. The examples below serve to illustrate this point.

Christ lag in Todesbanden

Durch Adams Fall ist ganz verderbt

J. S. Bach

At (1) the f is an accented passing tone. The harmonic function for the third and fourth beats of the first measure is dominant.

At (2) the c is an accented upper neighboring tone. The first and second beats of the last measure are in a dominant function.

The augmented triad, especially in the early part of the 18th century, is occasionally found as a fourth-classification triad in a minor key. It is invariably found in first inversion. During the latter part of the 18th century and during the 19th century, additional functional augmented triads appear as altered chords of the first and third classifications in a major key. As an altered chord the augmented triad is frequently found with the root in the bass. However, it must be remembered that the augmented triad is an infrequently encountered chord. When it does appear in the music, its normal progression is down a fifth to a major triad. The progression by elision up a second to the root of the subdominant is used almost as often.

SPELLING THE AUGMENTED TRIAD

To spell an augmented triad on any given root, spell the tone a major third above the root, spell the tone an augmented fifth (raise the perfect fifth a half-step) above the root, and spell the triad in the order of the root, third, and fifth. For example, spell the g-flat augmented triad. A major third above g-flat is b-flat; an augmented fifth above g-flat is d (the perfect fifth is d-flat); the g-flat augmented triad spelling is g♭ b♭ d.

EXERCISE 1. Be able to spell any augmented triad.
EXERCISE 2. Place the augmented triad on the staff, considering each given tone as the root.

EXERCISE 3. Play the augmented triad, considering each given tone as the root.

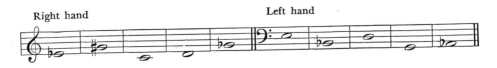

PLAYING THE AUGMENTED TRIAD

When the augmented triad has the root in the bass, the best tone to double is the root.

EXERCISE 4. Play any augmented triad in the position of the octave, third, or fifth. Example: Play the f-augmented triad in the position of the fifth.

The augmented triad with the root in the bass is usually found as an altered chord. The augmented triad V (dominant triad with raised-two) is one of the im-
$$\frac{\sharp}{2}$$

portant altered chords of the first classification during the 19th century. In the
progression V–I the voice leading is as follows:

$$\#\atop 2$$

Keep the common tone in the same voice, and the remaining upper voices move hv
step to the next triad tones.

EXERCISE 5. Play the progression V–I in any major key. Use the octave, third, or fifth in

$$\#\atop 2$$

the soprano of the dominant with raised-two.

When the augmented triad is in first inversion, the best tone to double is the
third.

EXERCISE 6. Play the first inversion of any augmented triad in the position of the octave,
third, or fifth.
Example: Play the first inversion of the d-augmented triad in the position
of the octave:

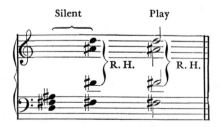

The first inversion of an augmented triad appears in the 18th and 19th centuries
as a **III** (fourth classification) in a minor key. Its normal progression is to **VI**.

$$\#\atop 7$$

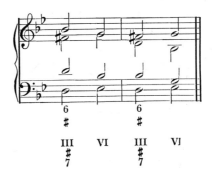

The movement of the voices in the progression III–VI is like the progression
$\begin{smallmatrix}\sharp\\7\end{smallmatrix}$

V–VI. The fifth of the augmented triad moves in tenths with the bass, and the
$\begin{smallmatrix}\sharp\\7\end{smallmatrix}$

remaining upper voices move contrary to the bass to the next chord tones.

EXERCISE 7. Use the first inversion of an augmented triad as a III in a minor key and play
$\begin{smallmatrix}\sharp\\7\end{smallmatrix}$

the progression III–VI.
$\begin{smallmatrix}\sharp\\7\end{smallmatrix}$

THE APPLICATION OF THE THEORY OF INVERSION

The augmented triad's root can be detected only by the classification of root movements. For this reason, the application of the theory of inversion will be taken up in Chapter 29—Chords of the Fourth Classification.

INTERVALS AND THE AUGMENTED TRIAD

The intervals which imply an augmented triad are listed in the following table:

Chord Members	Name of Interval
1 u 1	
3 u 3	
5 u 5	
	Perfect Octave
1 d 1	
3 d 3	
5 d 5	
1 u 5	
5 d 1	Augmented Fifth

Chord Members	Name of Interval
5 u 1⎫ 1 d 5⎭	Diminished Fourth
1 u 3; 3 d 1	Major Third
3 u 5; 5 d 3	Major Third
3 u 1; 1 d 3	Minor Sixth
5 u 3; 3 d 5	Minor Sixth

The intervals of the minor third, major sixth, perfect fourth, augmented fourth, perfect fifth, and diminished fifth cannot be used to imply an augmented triad.

The procedure established in Exercises 1 and 2 of Chapter 16 is to be followed in the next two exercises.

EXERCISE 8. Playing intervallic relationships in the augmented triad.
EXERCISE 9. Sing any intervallic relationship from a given pitch based on an augmented triad.

The augmented fifth is enharmonic with the minor sixth, and the diminished fourth is enharmonic with the major third. When dictating intervals based on an augmented triad, it will be necessary to supply the harmonic background. Otherwise, the intervals of the augmented fifth and diminished fourth will be identified as a minor sixth and major third, respectively. The procedure established in Exercises 15, 16, and 17 of Chapter 21 is to be followed in the next three exercises.

EXERCISE 10. Recognize from dictation the chord members and name of the interval based on an augmented triad.
EXERCISE 11. Intervals placed on the staff from dictation, based on an augmented triad.
EXERCISE 12. Recognize from dictation the following intervals and place them on the staff: octave, perfect fifth, diminished fifth,* perfect fourth, augmented fourth,* major third, minor third, augmented fifth,* diminished fourth,* major sixth, minor sixth, minor seventh, major second, and minor second.

---

* The harmonic background must be supplied for these intervals; otherwise, enharmonic solutions may appear.

Chapter 29

The Triad in the Fourth Classification: Mediant

The diatonic triad which is found in the fourth classification of major and minor keys is as follows:

Triad in the Fourth Classification

Major Key

Name	Symbol	Type Chord
Mediant	III	Minor Triad

Minor Key

Name	Symbol	Type Chord
Mediant with raised seven	III♯7	Augmented Triad
Mediant	III	Major Triad

The following examples illustrate the use of the mediant triads in a variety of musical textural styles during the 18th and 19th centuries:

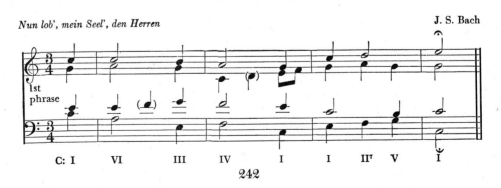

Nun lob', mein Seel', den Herren

J. S. Bach

Nun lasst uns Gott, dem Herren   J. S. Bach

3rd phrase

Bb: III   VI   IV   VII   I
       #5
                                    F: IV   V⁷ ———————————— I

Epitaphe d'un Paresseux   F. Couperin

C: II ———————————— V —— III—— VI II⁷ V —— I

Op. 40, No. 1   M. Clementi

IV   III   II   V   I

Sonata in E, Op. 109   L. von Beethoven

E: I ——— V —— VI — III —— IV — I —— V — I

Sonata in G, Op. 79   L. von Beethoven

G: I   V   VI   III   IV   I   V   I

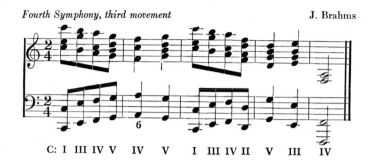

Fourth Symphony, third movement   J. Brahms

C: I III IV V   IV   V   I   III IV II   V   III   IV

PART-WRITING AND KEYBOARD: NORMAL PROGRESSION
AND ELISION

The mediant triad normally progresses down a fifth to the submediant triad.

Nun lob', mein' Seel, den Herren   J. S. Bach

5th phrase

A: III VI   IV   V ——————— I   I⁷   IV

In the following exercises the progression III to VI makes use of the two fundamental principles in part-writing two chords which have their roots a fifth apart.

Part-write the following:

Play at the keyboard the following:

In a minor key the mediant with seven-raised, III, appears most often in first

$$\overset{\#}{7}$$

inversion.   In this position, the composers invariably double the bass, the third of
the chord.   In the following example, compare the voice leading of the progression
V–VI with that of the progression III–VI.

$$\overset{\#}{7}$$

$$\overset{\#}{7}$$

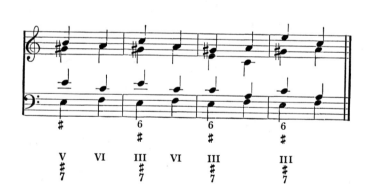

In comparing the two progressions, there is actually only one tone different, namely,
the b in the dominant triad is replaced by c in the mediant triad.

Part-write the following:

Play at the keyboard the following:

Composers use the elision of the fourth classification to the second classification as often as the normal progression. **III** to **IV** is more often encountered in musical analysis than **III** to **II**. One of the fundamental practical applications of the elision from the **III** is in connection with the harmonic treatment of the descending major scale or the natural minor scale.

Example:

Part-write the following:

Play at the keyboard the following:

The following exercises use the elision in a minor key:

EXERCISE 1. Be able to play at the keyboard the harmonization of the scale steps 8–7–6–5 in any major or natural minor key, as established in the previous drills.

HARMONIC DICTATION*

Characteristics:
> *a.* The triad in the fourth classification progresses normally to the chord
> of the third classification.
> *b.* Its root is on the mediant.

The harmonic dictation drills will be on the same order as those practised in Chapter 24.

Drill: A phrase will be played twice. As it is repeated, sing the root of each chord.

Drill: A phrase will be played twice. As it is repeated, identify orally or in writing the type of each chord. In writing, use A for augmented.

Drill: While you are singing the root of each chord in an exercise, the instructor may halt the phrase at any point. Sing the root of the chord to which you believe the last chord should progress.

> *Note:* If the root of the chord at the point at which the phrase was halted wants to progress to the root of a chord in the third classification, the chord belongs to the fourth classification.

Instructor plays:

Student sings:

4th Cl. 3rd Cl.

Drill: As a phrase is played at least three times, recite or write the classification of each chord.

I	Tonic	
1st Cl.	First Classification	
2nd Cl.	Second Classification	
3rd Cl.	Third Classification	
4th Cl.	Fourth Classification	

Drill: As a phrase is played three times, recite or write the name of each chord.

THE ELISION AND RETROGRESSION OF THE TRIAD IN THE FOURTH CLASSIFICATION

The elision III to IV is quite frequent. The retrogressions VI to III, IV to III, and II to III are occasionally encountered.

---

* The exercises for this section are found in the *Teachers Dictation Manual*, pages 74 through 79.

Drill: A phrase will be played twice. As it is repeated, recite or write the character of the harmonic movement.

Drill: As a phrase is played at least three times, recite or write the name of each chord.

Drill: As the instructor gives the key and plays the exercise at least three times, write the chord symbols, the soprano, and the figured bass on the staff.

PART-WRITING

The following exercises which make use of the mediant triad employ the part-writing principles introduced thus far.

Part-write the following:

There are a number of part-writing exceptions to triads having their roots a third apart. Compare the usual part-writing procedure with those found at (*a*) and (*b*) in the following examples.

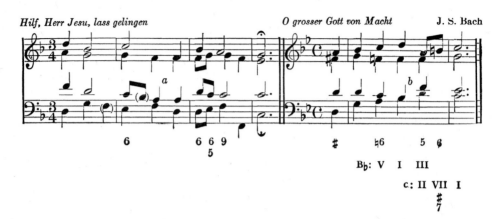

1. When a triad progresses down a third to another which has a doubled third:
   a. Keep two common tones; and the remaining upper voice will leap usually a fourth, rarely a fifth.

   b. Do not keep the common tones; move the third of the first in thirds or tenths with the bass, and the remaining voices contrary to the bass to the next chord tones.

2. When a triad progresses up a third to another which has a doubled third: Keep the fifth of the first triad and the third of the second triad as a common tone, move the third of the first triad in thirds or tenths with the bass, and the remaining voice will move by step to the next chord tone.

When these conventional exceptions are used, the chord progressions are I–VI, I–III, and IV–VI, and sometimes IV–II and V–III.

Part-write the following:

FOUR-VOICE SETTING OF A MELODY

EXERCISE 2. Use the following drills for the given melodies:

     Drill 1. Make at least two harmonizations. Compose at least two figured-bass counterpoints to each harmonization.

     Drill 2. Compose and part-write at least two settings.

EXERCISE 3. To the settings of 1, 2, 7, and 9 add an original consequent phrase which ends in a perfect authentic cadence.

EXERCISE 4. Compose in chorale style an original period, using the chords studied thus far.

1. $\frac{4}{4}$ meter in a minor key.   First phrase ends in a half-cadence.

2. $\frac{3}{4}$ meter in a major key.   First phrase ends in an imperfect authentic cadence.

Chapter 30

Introduction to Modulation
The Dominant and Subdominant Modulations

Modulation is a method of effecting change of key. The methods by which a new key may be established fall into two categories. The first category is concerned with the establishment of a new key at the initial announcement of a movement, section, period, phrase, or a sequential motive. The following examples illustrate the establishment of a new key at the initial announcement of a phrase:

The second category deals with the effect of changing from one key to another by means of chord progression occurring within the recitative, transition, development section, or phrase. Play the following examples.

At 1 the d-minor triad in c-major is a second-classification supertonic function. The third and fourth beat of this measure indicate a first-classification function in a-minor. The smoothness of the progression of the d-minor triad to the dominant effect on the e of the key of a-minor is made possible because the d-minor triad lost its function in the key of c and became a second-classification subdominant triad in a-minor. The d-minor triad is momentarily in two keys. The musical thought processes work in the following manner: first, the d-minor triad is thought of as a supertonic based on its approach; secondly, it is felt as a subdominant at the initial sounding of the dominant in a-minor.

At 2 the g-minor triad is momentarily in the keys of g-minor and b-flat major. It is the tonic function in g-minor and a submediant function in b-flat major. Here a rest chord becomes active, due to the fact that it is conceived of as a third-classification chord in b-flat major.

Common chord modulation occurs when the function of the first key can be supplanted by a function in the new key on a chord common to both keys. When the common chord is diatonic to both keys, the procedure is called *diatonic common chord modulation.*

When a new key is introduced by chromatic chord progression, the procedure is called *chromatic modulation.* This kind of harmonic movement is more forceful in its musical effect especially if the second chord in the chromatic progression cannot be logically analyzed in the first key. In the following example, which contains the chromatic progression, f-major triad to the d-major triad, note that both triads are first-classification dominants.

The f-major triad as a dominant is ready to move to the tonic in b-flat major. This feeling is destroyed by the chromatic movement to the d-major triad which is found to be a first-classification dominant triad in the key of g-minor.

A summary of the foregoing discussion may be best expressed in the following diagram:

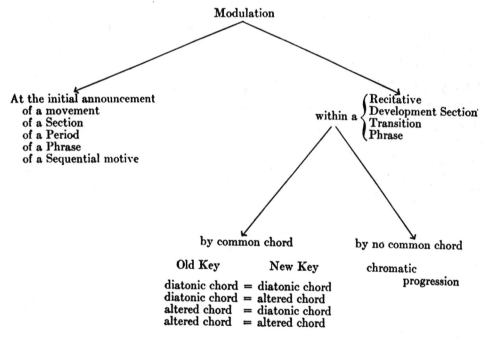

In the music of the 18th and 19th centuries, very little of real musical significance exists without modulation. The variety of harmonic interest achieved through the use of the classification of root movement did not provide sufficient harmonic material to satisfy completely the composer's sense of tonal interest. For this reason the composers felt the need for a variety of keys within a composition.

Analysis of the music clearly reveals that the composers used a concept of tonality which included not only the functions within an established basic key but likewise a variety of other keys which eventually gave way to this same established basic key. In a given composition, keys must bear a relationship to a basic key in much the same manner as chords in a key bear a relationship to their tonic center. Briefly, a composition has a generating tonal center.

Too many students formulate the opinion that a modulation to a new key destroys, obliterates, or effaces from the memory the old key. On the contrary, a modulation establishes a tonal relationship between the basic key and the new key. To confirm this idea, play the following example:

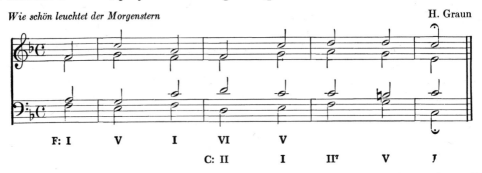

Wie schön leuchtet der Morgenstern   H. Graun

F: I   V   I   VI   V

C: II   I   II⁷   V   I

The example is the first phrase of a chorale which is in the key of f-major. The phrase contains a diatonic common chord modulation to the key of c-major. Is it not true that at the completion of the phrase, although the c-major triad feels like a tonic in c-major, the c-major triad still retains its dominant relationship to the key of f-major? The key of f-major is the basic key, and the key of c-major is in a secondary relationship to f-major. For this reason, the harmonic movement is defined as a diatonic common chord modulation to the dominant key of c-major.

Major and minor key relationships are explained by the Circle of Fifths.

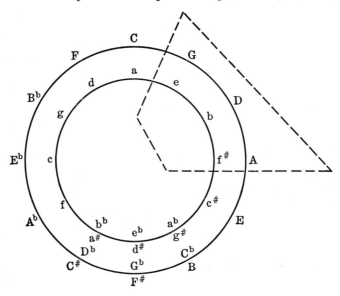

If one progresses to the right in either circle, the next key will have one sharp more or one flat less than the previous key; similarly, if one progresses to the left, the next key will have one flat more or one sharp less than the previous key. If a quadrangle is placed about three keys in the major circle and the corresponding three minor keys in the minor circle, as shown, the enclosed major and minor tonic triads include all the possible diatonic triads in the major key of the center major triad, or in the minor key of the center minor triad.

For example, select d-major as the center. The following is the result:

Position in			Position in
	Major Circle		
	Minor Circle		
D Major			D Major
II	Minor triad – – – – – – – – – e	G – – – – – Major triad	IV
VI	Minor triad – – – – – – – – – b	D – – – – – Major triad	I
III	Minor triad – – – – – – – – – f#	A – – – – – Major triad	V

Examining the Circle of Fifths, we see that d-major and b-minor have the same signature. Since d-major is considered the starting harmonic center, each of the remaining keys has either the same signature, one sharp more, or one sharp less. In addition, the tonic triad of each key is found as a diatonic triad of the key of d-major.

If the tonic triad of the new key is found as a diatonic triad in the original key, the modulation is said to be a *Closely Related Key*. If a modulation takes place to a closely related key, the new key derives its name according to the *position of its tonic in the original key*. For example, if a modulation takes place from d-major to e-minor, the modulation is to the supertonic key.

MODULATION TO THE DOMINANT AND SUBDOMINANT

Remembering that in a major key the dominant and subdominant triads are major and that in the natural minor key the dominant and subdominant triads are minor, study the following modulation table:

Original Key		Closely Related Key	
	Interval between Tonics	Type of Key	Name of Key
Major	Up a perfect fifth	Major	Dominant
	Down a perfect fifth	Major	Subdominant
Minor	Up a perfect fifth	Minor	Dominant
	Down a perfect fifth	Minor	Subdominant

KEYBOARD

COMMON CHORD MODULATION

Define the type of modulation and give the harmonic analysis of the following exercises which are to be solved at the keyboard:

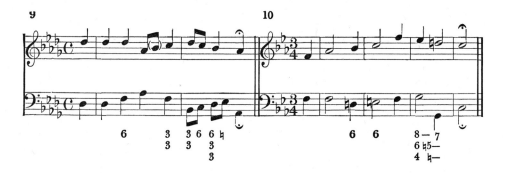

CHROMATIC MODULATION

A chromatic progression, as distinguished from a diatonic progression, is one which has in the second chord a chromatic inflection of a note or notes common to both chords.

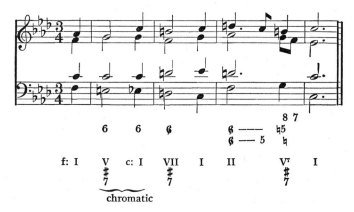

In the example above, the chromatic inflection of e to the e-flat in the bass as the c-major triad changes to the c-minor triad identifies this progression as chromatic. The c-major triad is a V in f-minor; the c-minor triad is conceived as a I in c-minor.

$$\overset{\sharp}{7}$$

There is no common chord which one can analyze as functional in both keys.

Define the type of modulation and give the harmonic analysis of the following exercises which are to be solved at the keyboard:

HARMONIC DICTATION *

Drill: A phrase is played once. Determine the interval between the root of the original tonic and the root of the new tonic, and the character of the new tonic triad. Example:

Instructor plays:

Students sings on a neutral syllable:

Student recites: Up a perfect fifth to a major key. Modulation to the dominant

Drill: The instructor names the original key and plays the phrase once. Sing with the names of the notes the root of the original tonic and the root of the new tonic, and the pitch names of the new tonic triad. This is followed by reciting the name of the interval relating the tonics, and by naming the modulation.

* The exercises for this section are found in the *Teachers Dictation Manual*, pages 80 through 86, 90, and 91.

Example:

Instructor names the original
   key and plays:

Student sings with
   pitch names:

Student recites: Up a perfect fifth to a-major, dominant key

Drill: The original key is given, and the phrase is played four times.
    Write the chord symbols, the soprano, and the figured bass on the staff.
    Example. Original key is c-major:

Instructor plays four times:

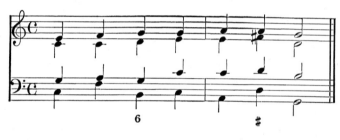

Student's solution:

      C: I   IV   V   I

                  G: IV   II   V   I

    Example.   Original key is f-minor:

Instructor plays four times:

Student's solution:

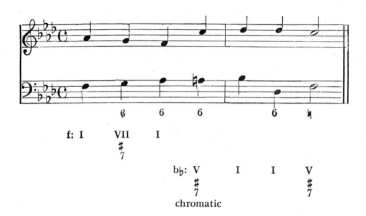

MELODIC ANALYSIS AND SIGHT-SINGING

Melodies which contain more than one key make use of the two basic modulatory procedures outlined on pages 253.   In the *Sight-Singing Manual*, #81 and #82 are small three-part forms, namely A B A.   The A's are in the basic key, and the B's are in the dominant key.   The dominant key is established at the initial announcement of B; likewise, at the initial announcement of the return of A, the basic key is re-established.   No common chord modulation is to be found in either #81 or #82.   The rest of the analysis will be conducted in the same manner as in former chapters.

Common chord modulation is to be analyzed in the following manner:

The instructor is to assign for analysis Exercises 1, 4, 6, 10, and 14. After these exercises have been discussed, use the remaining exercises for sight-singing.

1 *Die Feldflasche*   R. Keller
   Adagio

2 *Gesang Ausziehender Krieger*   A. Methfessel
   Moderato

3   C. P. E. Bach
   Adagio

4   J. Kirnberger
   Allegro

5   G. Handel
   Moderato

6   J. Eberlin
   Andante

7   J. S. Bach
Larghetto

8   J. Albrechtsberger
Moderato

9   A. Romberg
Allegro

10   A. Klengel
Moderato

11   N. Sala
Andante

12   J. E. Bach
Adagio

13   *Die Lore am Thore*   Folksong
Moderato

14 *Mädel, 's ist Winter*
    Andante
                                              A. Methfessel

15 *Der Lebenslauf*
    Allegro
                                              R. Keller

Further sight-singing exercises are found in the *Sight-Singing Manual* as follows: 81, 82, 83, 84, 89, 97, 107, 116, 121, 122, 146, 154, 155, 160, 165, 175, 190, 192, 219.

MELODIC DICTATION*

The student's completed melodic dictation is not to be considered finished unless it is accompanied by the implied harmonic analysis showing how the modulations took place.

* Suitable melodic dictation exercises may be found in the *Teachers Dictation Manual*, page 29 through 32, exercises 69 through 94.

MELODIC COMPOSITION

In Appendix III Binary and Ternary Forms are defined.

EXERCISE 1. Compose at least two Binary melodies:
        In the style of a folksong
        In the style of a late 17th century dance form
EXERCISE 2. Compose at least two Ternary melodies:
        In the style of a symphonic theme
        In the style of an art song

FOUR-VOICE SETTING OF A CHORALE

EXERCISE 3. Use the following drills for the given melodies:
        Drill 1. Make at least two harmonizations. Compose at least two figured-
            bass counterpoints to each harmonization.
        Drill 2. Compose and part-write at least two settings.

* In the first phrase, use a half cadence on the subdominant in the subdominant key. See *Contrapuntal Harmonic Technique*, by McHose, p. 299.

EXERCISE 4. In chorale style compose a period in which a modulation to the dominant or subdominant occurs at the end of the first phrase.

Chapter 31

Modulation to Closely Related Keys
(Continued)

✥

Study the following modulation table:

Original Key		Closely Related Key	
	Interval between Tonics	Type of Key	Name of Key
	Up a major third	Minor	Mediant
Major	Down a minor third	Minor	Submediant
	Up a major second	Minor	Supertonic
	Up a minor third	Major	Mediant
Minor	Down a major third	Major	Submediant
	Down a major second	Major	Subtonic

PART-WRITING AND KEYBOARD

The exercises which follow introduce no new problems in part-writing. The instructor will select the exercises which are to be used for part-writing. The remaining exercises are to be completed at the keyboard. Each exercise is to be given a harmonic analysis.

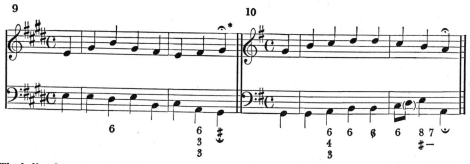

* The half cadence, containing IV-V with soprano line 6→5, or the first inversion of IV→V with soprano
line 4→5, is called the phrygian cadence. See 2→1 and 7→8 of phrygian mode, Chapter 32, page 273.

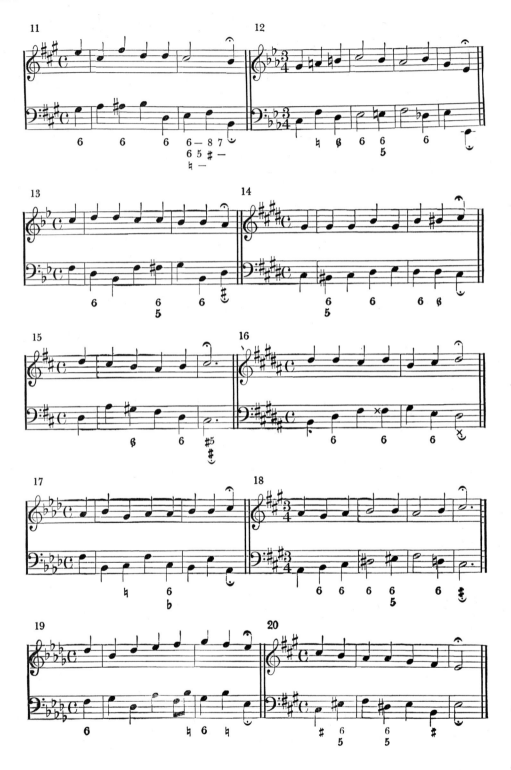

HARMONIC DICTATION*

Drill: A phrase is played once. Determine the interval between the root of the original tonic and the root of the new tonic, and the character of the new tonic.

Drill: The instructor names the original key and plays the phrase once. Sing with the names of the notes the root of the original tonic and the root of the new tonic, and the pitch names of the new tonic triad. This is to be followed by reciting the name of the interval relating the tonics, and by naming the modulation.

Drill: The original key is given, and the phrase is played four times. Write the chord symbols, showing the common chord modulation or chromatic modulation as the case may be, the soprano, and the figured bass on the staff.

MELODIC ANALYSIS AND SIGHT-SINGING

In accordance with the procedure followed previously, a number of exercises are to be selected for analysis before sight-singing is stressed. Exercises involving modulation to the closely related keys stressed in this chapter are found in the *Sight-Singing Manual,* according to the following numbers:† 87, 88, 90, 91, 92, 93, 94, 95, 96, 98, 99, 100, 103, 104, 105, 106, 123, 124, 128, 129, 130, 147, 151, 153, 158, 162, 164, 168, 172, 176, 177, 178, 180, 194, 198, 206, 218, 223, 225, 228, 229, 230, 231, 233, 234, 235, 237, 238, 240, 248.

MELODIC DICTATION‡

Melodic dictation will be practised in the same way as in former chapters.

ORIGINAL WORK

1. Compose in four voices a phrase which contains a modulation to a closely related key.
2. Compose melodies using a double period form which contain at least two modulations to closely related keys.

---

* Exercises found in *Teachers Dictation Manual,* pages 87 through 89, and 92 through 95.

† Modulation to dominant or subdominant may also be found in these exercises, in addition to the modulations stressed in this chapter.

‡ Melodic dictation exercises suitable for this chapter are found in the *Teachers Dictation Manual,* beginning on page 32, Exercises 95 through 119.

Chapter 32
The Modes

Some of the hymns for congregational participation in the Catholic and Protestant churches during the 18th and 19th centuries have melodies which do not conform to the conventional major and minor scales. The composers, however, gave them a harmonic treatment which employed the principles of the classification of root movement. The chorale melody, *Nun komm der Heiden Heiland*, composed by Martin Luther and found in the "Erfurter Enchiridion" (1524), is as follows:

Bach's treatment of Luther's chorale is as follows:

Bach's setting is definitely in the key of a-minor. The analysis of each phrase is as

272

follows: first phrase is in a-minor; second phrase opens in a-minor and modulates to c-major, the phrase ending on a half cadence on the subdominant triad; the entire third phrase is in a-minor; the last phrase begins in e-minor and modulates to a-minor, the phrase ending in a-minor and using the *Tierce de Picardie* in the last chord.

In Bach's cantata No. 61, *Nun komm, der Heiden Heiland*, the opening chorus uses the same chorale melody. Bach changes the g-natural in the first phrase and closing phrase to a g-sharp, thus making the entire melody sound like a conventional melody of the 18th century. The four-voice setting of the last phrase is as follows:

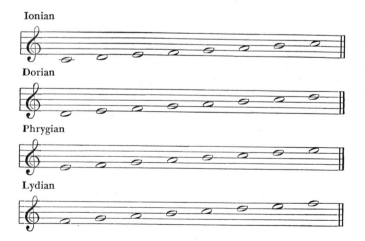

Many melodies were carried into the 18th and 19th centuries which were originally in the character of the old church modes (Gregorian classification). Examples show the manner in which melodic lines can be transformed and lose their original character. Such well-known chorales as *Vater Unser im Himmelreich*, *Jesu meine Freude*, and others lost their original character by the middle of the 18th century; yet a chorale like *O Haupt voll Blut und Wunden* retained its original melodic character.*

Although at the time of Martin Luther the chorale melodies which he and his contemporaries composed were undoubtedly classified according to the conventional Gregorian modal table, by the time of Bach these same melodies may be classified in one of six modes.

Ionian

Dorian

Phrygian

Lydian

---

* See *The Contrapuntal Harmonic Technique of the 18th Century*, by A. I. McHose, Chapter 32.

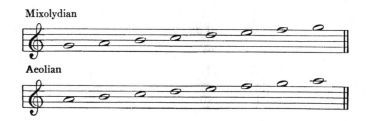

The tone upon which the mode is built is called the final. The signature for each of the above modes does not contain any accidentals. If the final of each mode is placed on the staff, the result will be Guido's Hexachord.*

The final of each mode then has a definite position in the hexachord. The dorian's final is the second tone of the hexachord; the phrygian's final is the third tone; and so on. Bach and his contemporaries transposed the modes based on the hexachord system of transposition. If the hexachord is transposed to "a," note the signature and the position of the finals in the following example:

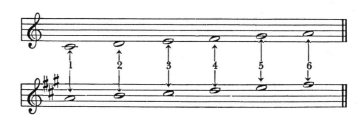

In accord with this method of obtaining the modal signature, a musician who wishes to write a phrygian melody with a final note on g will use the following procedure: the final of the phrygian mode is found as the third tone of the hexachord. Consequently, g is the third tone of the hexachord built on e-flat. The signature will then be three flats.

EXERCISE 1. Place the signature on the staff for the following modes:

1. dorian on e
2. mixolydian on f
3. lydian on a
4. phrygian on f
5. dorian on g
6. mixolydian on e
7. mixolydian on b-flat
8. phrygian on g-sharp
9. lydian on e-flat
10. phrygian on c

* See page 104.

It is necessary for the musician to recognize a second method of deriving a modal signature. This method appeared during the last half of the 19th century. The aural effect of the modal melodies was classified into two groups: those which were predominantly major and those which were predominantly minor.* The composers observed that lydian and mixolydian differed from the ionian (major) in only one tone. In like manner, the dorian and phrygian differed from the aeolian (natural minor) in only one tone. The analysis of this concept is as follows:

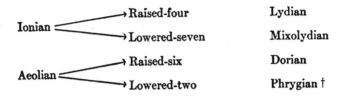

In this interpretation of the modes the alteration is called the characteristic tone. The signature used in this method of notating a mode uses the signature for either the ionian or the aeolian mode, and the accidental appears before the characteristic note. For example, the dorian melody which has its final note on F would have the signature of f-minor (four flats), and the raised-six would always be indicated by a natural. Accordingly, the lydian on E would have the signature of four sharps, and the characteristic note would be a-sharp.

EXERCISE 2. Place the signature and the characteristic note on the staff for the following modes:

    1. phrygian on d   6. dorian on g
    2. dorian on f-sharp   7. mixolydian on c
    3. lydian on a   8. lydian on f-sharp
    4. lydian on d-flat   9. phrygian on f
    5. mixolydian on e   10. mixolydian on e-flat

EXERCISE 3. Sing a modal scale, using a neutral syllable.
    The instructor plays any pitch and directs the student to use it as the first tone of any one of the six modes. The student determines whether the given mode is basically major or minor, and locates the characteristic tone. For example: sing the lydian mode. Feel an ionian modal scale; then sing that modal scale, raising the fourth degree one half-step.

EXERCISE 4. Spell a modal scale.
    The instructor designates the mode and its final. The student determines whether the basic spelling will be ionian or aeolian, locates its characteristic note, and spells the mode.
    Example: Spell the dorian mode on f-sharp.
        Spell the f-sharp aeolian scale with raised-sixth. f♯ g♯ a b c♯ d♯ e f♯

---

* Gioseffe Zarlino in the 16th century suggested a re-classification of the modes based upon the size of the third above the final.

† If the fifth of the phrygian mode is lowered a half-step, one may obtain the locrian mode. 18th and 19th century composers did not use this mode.

EXERCISE 5. Play a modal scale.

The instructor designates the mode. Determine whether the mode is basically ionian or aeolian, locate the characteristic tone, and play the mode. Example: Play the mixolydian mode on e-flat.

Play the e-flat ionian mode with lowered-seven.

EXERCISE 6. Determine the mode of each of the following examples:

Mazurka, Op. 24, No. 2   F. Chopin

Romeo and Juliette   P. Tschaikowsky

Mazurka, Op. 33, No. 2   F. Chopin

And I Will Exalt Him (Israel in Egypt)   G. Handel

Symphonie in E minor

J. Brahms

The Coasts of High Barbary

English Folksong

Allegro

Dabbling in the Dew

English Folksong

Adagio

* Change back to E major occurs here.

The Husbandman and Servingman

Andante

Folk Tune of Brittany

Allegro

Folk Tune from Brittany

𝅗𝅥. = 82

Gently, Johnny My Jingalo   **English Folksong**

Adagio

Henry Martin   **English Folksong**

Allegretto

EXERCISE 7. Sight-singing.

Turn to the *Sight-Singing Manual*, Section X. At the completion of each sight-singing exercise be sure to identify the mode. For further exercises turn to the *Folk Song Sight-Singing Series:*—

Book VI, 30 through 41

Book VII, 9, 14, 26, 34, 48, 61, 63, 65, 76, 89

EXERCISE 8. Melodic dictation.*

The dictation procedure is the same as in former chapters.

* Melodic dictation exercises for this chapter are found in the *Teachers Dictation Manual*, pages 37 through 40.

Chapter 33

Foreign Modulation; Change of Mode

A foreign modulation occurs when the new key's signature differs from that of the original key by two or more accidentals. Situations in which diatonic common chords may be used to promote foreign modulation are meager. In the following example, Mozart uses the dominant seventh chord as the common chord in accomplishing the foreign modulation, C-major to C-minor:

Sonata in F Major

W. Mozart

C: I   V   c: I   V   I

The V⁷ in C-major is likewise the V⁷ in C-minor. Modulation involving the *paral-*

$$\begin{array}{c}\sharp\\7\end{array}$$

*lel relationship** between a major and a minor key is called *change of mode*.

In the following example the first phrase ends in a half-cadence in the key of G-major. The second phrase opens in the key of G-minor and returns to G-major. These parallel keys are brought close together by the fact that the dominant chord in each key is the same sound.

---

* Parallel related chords are those which contain the same basic spelling but which differ in the accidental spelling; for example, C E G and c e♭ g.

Der Tod Jesu, No. 3   C. Graun

The system of keys resulting from parallel relationship can be expanded to twelve keys, as shown in the following diagram:

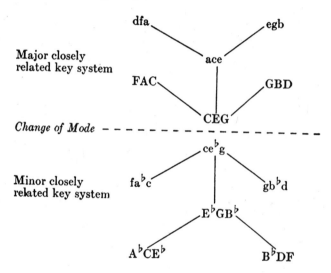

The foreign key receives its name based on its relation to the original key. If a modulation takes place from C-major, or any of its closely related keys, to B-flat major, the new key is defined as "a foreign modulation by change of mode to the subtonic key of B-flat major." Conversely, if a modulation occurs from the basic key of C-minor to D-minor, it is defined as "a foreign modulation by change of mode to the supertonic key of D-minor."

On the following pages you will find Mozart's *Das Veilchen (The Violet)*, followed by a diagram of its key scheme. While the melody is being played, the student is to follow the arrows which indicate the manner in which the modulations are carried out.

* I is an augmented triad, and it is classified in the key of G-major as an altered chord. An altered chord
♯
5
must satisfy two requirements:
  1. Its spelling must contain raised or lowered degrees of the key;
  2. It must retain the function of the basic diatonic chord shown from which it is derived. See *Contrapuntal Harmonic Technique*, Chapter 22.

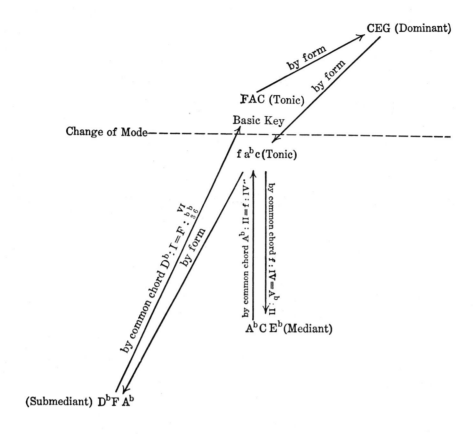

MELODIC ANALYSIS AND SIGHT-SINGING

EXERCISE 1. Sight-sing and make the key scheme for the following melodies:

Der Gott und die Bajadere K. Zelter

2 Allegro

Lament and Weep C. H. Graun

3 Andante

Wonne der Wehmuth L. von Beethoven
4 *Andante espressivo*

Der Blumenkranz F. Mendelssohn
5 *Andante con moto*

Das erste Veilchen   F. Mendelssohn
6 *Andante con moto*

Gebet   C. von Weber
7 *Adagio ma non troppo*

Der Liebwürtige — C. von Weber

Further sight-singing exercises containing foreign modulation are found in the *Sight-Singing Manual*, Section VIII, Exercises 250 through 259, also Exercises 260 and 261.

MELODIC DICTATION*

Melodic dictation will be practised in the same way as in former chapters.

* Melodic dictation exercises suitable for this chapter are found in the *Teachers Dictation Manual*, beginning on page 43, Exercises 147 through 153.

ppendix 1

Figured Bass Symbols

Beginning in the late 16th century and extending through the 18th century, there existed a practice of using symbols in connection with the bass voice to indicate harmonic structures and horizontal movement of the voices above the bass. This practice is called *Thorough-Bass* or *Figured Bass*. By the 18th century, musicians had worked out a universal system of symbols.

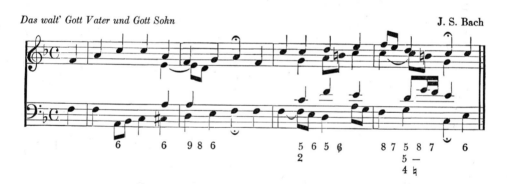

The symbol system for the triad with its root in the bass is as follows:

1. The bass note without any symbol indicates the root position of a triad. The notes of the chord will be in relation to the signature of the key in which the bass is found.

2. The flat, sharp, or natural sign is used to obtain chord spellings which would otherwise be impossible to get, due to the signature. When the sign appears directly beneath the bass, the note a third or tenth above the bass note is altered accordingly. Sometimes an Arabic numberal 3 with a line through it, ⅔, is used. This indicates that the note a third or tenth above the bass is to be raised one half-step.

3. Occasionally the fifth of the chord must be indicated for functional reasons. The ♭5, ♮5, or 5̷ indicates lowering or raising the note a fifth or an octave and a fifth (a twelfth) above the bass note.

4. If the pitch of both the third and the fifth above the bass note is to be altered, two symbols are used below the bass note, the lower symbol referring to the third and the upper to the fifth.

5. The complete figuration written below the bass tone to indicate the first inversion of a triad is 6.   Under normal conditions the 3 is omitted.
   3

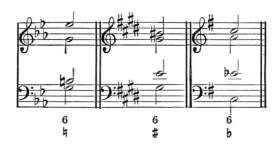

6. When a ♭, ♮, ♯, or ♯ is placed below the 6, the third or tenth above the bass note is affected.

7. Sometimes just a 6 with a line drawn diagonally through it, ₲, is used. This raises by one half-step the note a sixth above the bass note or an octave and a sixth above the bass note.

Appendix 2

A. TEMPO TERMS

Accelerando (Accel.)......... gradual increase of the established tempo

Adagietto.................... a tempo slightly faster than adagio

Adagio...................... a tempo slower than andante and faster than largo

Adagissimo................. very slow

Allargando.................. gradual decrease of the tempo

Allegretto (Allgtt⁰.).......... a tempo between allegro and andante

Allegro (All⁰.).............. quick tempo

Andante (Andᵗᵉ.)............ a moderate tempo

Andantino (Andⁿ⁰.)......... usually understood to mean slightly slower than andante

A tempo.................... return to the original tempo

Grave...................... slow and solemn

Langsam................... slowly

Largando................... same as allargando

Larghetto.................. a tempo slightly faster than largo

Largo...................... in a very slow tempo; broad in character

Leggiero (Legg.)........... light, airy

Lento..................... a tempo faster than larghetto and slower than andante

L'istesso tempo............ same tempo

Maestoso.................. majestic, dignified

Moderato (Mod.).......... tempo of a moderate pace between andante and allegro

Modéré.................... moderately

Non tanto; non troppo...... a prefixed term meaning "not too"; for example, "non troppo allegro" means not too quick a tempo

Plus lent.................. more slowly

Presto.................... a very fast tempo, faster than an allegro

Prestissimo............... as fast as possible

Rallentando (Rall.)......... growing slower and slower

Ritardando (Ritard.)........ gradual decrease of the established tempo

Rubato.................... a term meaning unsteady tempo. This is accomplished by slight accelerandos and ritardandos. See a musical dictionary for an artistic explanation of the term.

Stringendo (String.)......... quickening the tempo

Vivace (Viv.).............. lively tempo; fast tempo

B. OTHER COMMON MUSICAL TERMS

Agitato.................... excited

Alla breve................ $\frac{4}{4}$ conducted in "two" $\mathbb{C} = \frac{2}{2}$

Allegramente.............. brightly

Assai..................... very

Assez..................... fairly

Brio (con)................ (with) spirit

Deciso.................... decided, energetic

Dolce (Dol.).............. sweetly

Dolcissimo (Dolcis.)...... very sweet

Dolente................... doleful

Energico.................. energetically

Espressivo (Esp., Espr.,

    Express.).............. with expression

Gracieux.................. gracefully

Grazioso (Graz.).......... gracefully

Hastig.................... impetuous

Incalzando................ pressing forward

Inquieto.................. restless

Klagend................... lamenting

Leicht.................... light

Leist..................... soft

Lieto..................... joyous

Lievemente................ lightly

Mächtig................... powerful

Mässig.................... moderate

Mancante.................. dying away

Movente................... moving

Nettement................. clearly

Non....................... not

Perdendo.................. gradually dying away

Pesante................... heavy

Pianamente................ softly

Piangendo................. plaintive

Più....................... more

Placido................... peaceful

Poco...................... little

Poussez................... speed up

Quasi..................... almost

Rasch..................... fast

Rauschend................. exuberant

Reprendere................ return to the original tempo

Risoluto.................. resolute

Ruhig..................... quiet

Scherzando (Scherz.)...... playful

Segue (Seg.).............. follows

Sehr...................... very
Sempre (Sem., Semp.)........ always
Senza..................... without
Smorzando (Smorz.)......... dying away
Strepitoso................. noisy
Subito.................... without pause; abrupt change
Tanto..................... much
Teneramente............... tenderly
Timoroso.................. timidly
Traîné.................... dragged
Tranquillo................ quietly
Très...................... very
Troppo.................... too much
Unruhig................... restless
Vaghezza, con............. with charm
Vite...................... quick
Volante................... swift
Vorwärtz.................. faster
Wuchtig................... forceful
Zu........................ to
Zurückhalten.............. to hold back

$\mathcal{A}$ppendix 3

Elementary Forms of 18th and 19th Century Music

THE PHRASE

A *phrase* is the fundamental unit of musical form.   In the course of a composition one identifies phrases by their cadences.   Phrases vary in length.   In 18th and 19th century music a phrase is usually found to be two, four, or eight measures in length.   Phrases of one, three, five, or seven are not infrequent.   The tempo of the music tends to develop a natural feeling for a phrase.

Phrases are classified and named depending on the beat or part of the beat of the measure in which they originate and terminate.

A *masculine phrase* begins on a heavy beat.

A *feminine phrase* begins on a light beat or a fractional part of a beat.

Phrases which end on a heavy beat have a masculine ending.

Phrases which end on a light beat have a feminine ending.

Complete understanding of the form of a phrase depends upon its beginning and ending. There are, therefore, four types of phrase forms:

1. A masculine phrase with a masculine ending
2. A masculine phrase with a feminine ending
3. A feminine phrase with a masculine ending
4. A feminine phrase with a feminine ending

A *figure* is a small grouping of notes capable of being identified as a basis from which the phrase is created. A figure may contain as few as two notes.

A *motive* or *motif*. Percy Scholes, in his *The Oxford Companion to Music*, considers a figure and a motive to mean the same in considering the structure of music. Willi Apel, in his *Harvard Dictionary of Music*, does not agree.*

---

* See *Harvard Dictionary of Music* (Cambridge, Massachusetts, Harvard University Press, 1947).

Phrases may be modified in length by *extension*.

LARGER FORMAL UNITS

A *period* is the natural grouping of two phrases. The first phrase is called the antecedent (announcing phrase). The second phrase of a period is called the consequent (answering phrase). In a period the answering phrase does not have to be similar in melodic and rhythmic content to the antecedent phrase.

A *double period* is grouping of two periods. For an example see *Sight-Singing Manual*, #3.

Binary Form. Two-part form means that the music gives the impression of being divided into two parts. The parts are designated as A and B. The size of the A or B may be a phrase, a period, or even a double period in length. Key relationships play an important rôle in clarifying two-part form. 17th and early 18th century compositions contain the best examples of two-part form. Short pieces by later composers often use this form. For an example of two-part form see *Sight-Singing Manual*, #70. A is a period, and B is a repeated period. In this form, B usually begins in a related key and ends in the original key.

Ternary Form. Three-part form means that the music divides itself into three parts, namely, A, B, A. B is usually in contrast to A, in possibly either different character or in a different key. The latter is the most common procedure. For examples, see *Sight-Singing Manual*, #81 and #82.

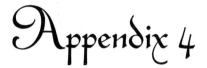

Appendix 4

Other Scales

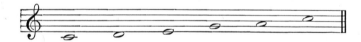

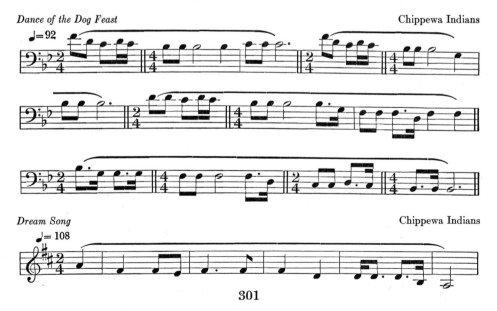

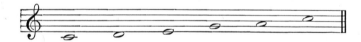

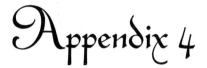

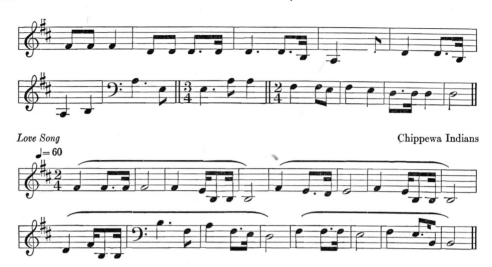

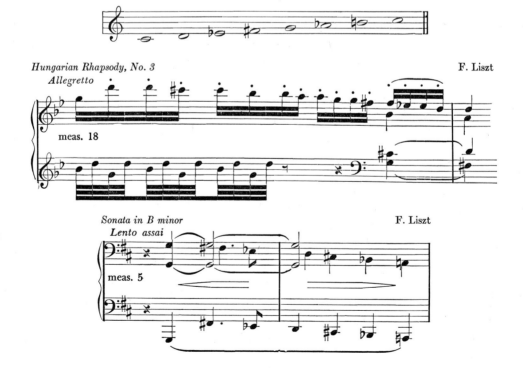

Hungarian Rhapsody, No. 3   F. Liszt

Sonata in B minor   F. Liszt

Appendix 4

Other Scales

❧

PENTATONIC SCALE

A pentatonic scale contains five notes in each octave. Compared with the scales used in the 18th and 19th century compositions, a pentatonic scale is commonly referred to as a "Gapped Scale." Use of the pentatonic scales can be traced back as far as 2000 B.C. in China. In our own country, Indian and many Negro melodies are pentatonic. In like manner, there are many folk melodies of Scotland which are fundamentally pentatonic. The most common pentatonic scale is as follows:

The following musical examples employ the pentatonic scale:

Dance of the Dog Feast — Chippewa Indians

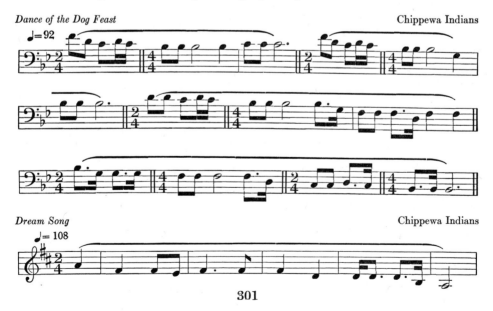

Dream Song — Chippewa Indians

301

Love Song   Chippewa Indians

For examples of pentatonic melodies, see *Sight-Singing Manual*, #189, #199, #204.

HUNGARIAN MINOR SCALE

The Hungarian minor or "Gypsy Scale" is the harmonic minor scale with the raised fourth degree.   The scale contains two augmented seconds, 3–4 and 6–7. The following musical examples employ the Gypsy scale.

Hungarian Dance   J. Brahms

Molto sostenuto

WHOLE-TONE SCALE

The whole-tone scale is composed of six notes within an octave, each tone being equidistant from the other. Accordingly, there are actually only two different sounding whole-tone scales possible in equal temperament.

Before the late 19th century there are very few examples of the whole-tone scales in use.

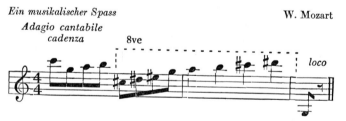

Ein musikalischer Spass   W. Mozart

Adagio cantabile
cadenza

The whole-tone scale appears infrequently by the middle of the 19th century.

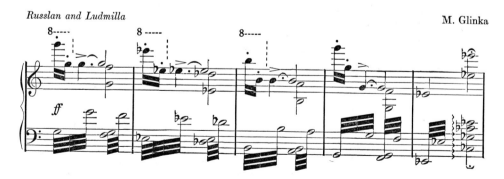

Russlan and Ludmilla   M. Glinka

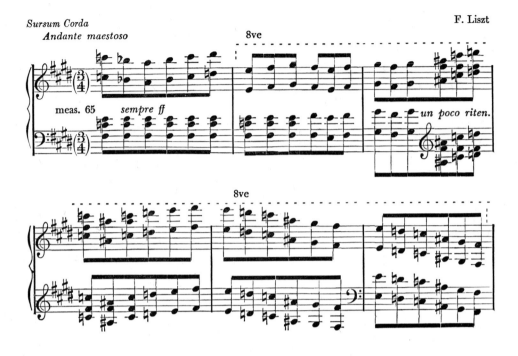

CHROMATIC SCALE

The chromatic scale within the octave makes use of all of the twelve tones, either ascending or descending. When the chromatic scale is composed of harmonic and non-harmonic tones, the composers notate the scale as follows:

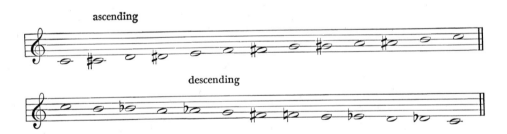

When the tones of the chromatic scale are harmonic, the composers notate, for example, the chromatic tones of the key of C as follows:

Examples of extended chromatic scales are frequently encountered on dominant function.

Appendix 5

Acoustics of Chords and Scales

CHORDS

In the natural scale the best ratios for determining the frequencies of the respective chord members of major and minor triads are found as follows:

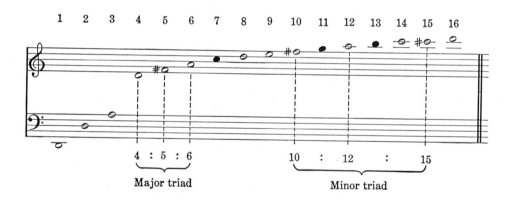

In the major triad, the major third's ratio is 5/4; the minor third's ratio is 6/5.

In the minor triad, the minor third's ratio is 12/10, which is actually 6/5; the major third's ratio is 15/12, which is actually 5/4.

The factor for the major third's ratio 5/4 is 1.25.

The factor for the minor third's ratio 6/5 is 1.2.

To determine in the natural scale the best ratios for the diminished triad and the augmented triad, it is necessary to obtain ratios which will approximate as closely as possible the factors of the major and minor thirds.

By extending the natural scale up to its thirty-second harmonic, suitable ratios for the diminished and augmented triads can be found as follows.

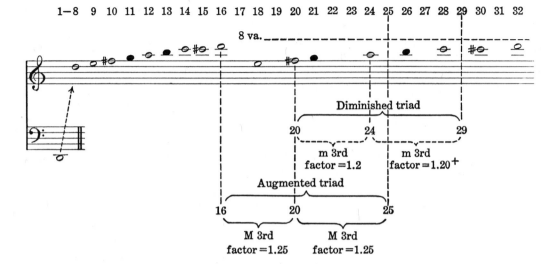

The diminished triad's ratio will be 20:24:29.

The augmented triad's ratio will be 16:20:25.

The major-minor seventh chord's best ratio is found by adding the best ratio of a minor third above a major triad. Accordingly, the best ratio for the major-minor seventh chord is 16:20:24:29.

SCALES

The physicist derives his diatonic major scale in much the same manner as Rameau. He points out that the natural diatonic major scale is built upon three major triads whose roots are in a perfect fifth arrangement.

Tonic	$c^1 : e^1 : g^1$	
Dominant	$g^1 : b^1 : d^2$	$4 : 5 : 6$
Subdominant	$f^1 : a^1 : c^2$	

Considering c^1 as the fundamental of the key, vibration ratios can be obtained as follows:

$$c^2 = 2\,c^1$$
$$e^1 = \tfrac{5}{4}\,c^1$$
$$g^1 = \tfrac{3}{2}\,c^1$$

$b^1 = \tfrac{5}{4}\,g^1$ but g^1 is $\tfrac{3}{2}\,c^1$; then in terms of c^1; $b^1 = \tfrac{5}{4} \times \tfrac{3}{2}\,e^1 = \tfrac{15}{8}\,c^1$

$d^2 = $ fifth plus fifth above $c^1 = \tfrac{3}{2} \times \tfrac{3}{2}\,c^1 = \tfrac{9}{4}\,c^1$;

$\qquad d^2$ is $2d^1$; therefore $2d^1 = \tfrac{9}{4}\,c^1$; $d^1 = \tfrac{9}{8}\,c^1$

$f^1 = $ a perfect fifth below c; knowing c^1 and c^2, we may obtain f^1

$\qquad$ by subtracting a fifth from the octave; fourth above $c^1 = f^1$

$$= \frac{2}{\tfrac{3}{2}}\,c^1 = \tfrac{4}{3}\,c^1$$

$a^1 = \tfrac{5}{4}\,f^1$, but f^1 is $\tfrac{4}{3}\,c^1$; then $a^1 = \tfrac{5}{4} \times \tfrac{4}{3}\,c^1 = \tfrac{5}{3}\,c^1$

To summarize the previous calculations based on c^1, the frequencies of any of the tones in the key of C-major may be obtained by using the following ratios for each tone:

Frequency	264	297	330	352	396	440	495	528
	c^1	d^1	e^1	f^1	g^1	a^1	b^1	c^2
Ratio	1	$\frac{9}{8}$	$\frac{5}{4}$	$\frac{4}{3}$	$\frac{3}{2}$	$\frac{5}{3}$	$\frac{15}{8}$	2

The interval ratio for obtaining any tone above or below any scale tone is as follows:

$$d^1 \text{ to } e^1 \text{ is } c^1e^1 - c^1d^1 = \frac{\frac{5}{4}}{\frac{9}{8}} = \frac{5}{4} \times \frac{8}{9} = \frac{10}{9}$$

$$e^1f^1 \text{ is } c^1f^1 - c^1e^1 = \frac{\frac{4}{3}}{\frac{5}{4}} = \frac{4}{3} \times \frac{4}{5} = \frac{16}{15}$$

$$f^1g^1 \text{ is } c^1g^1 - c^1f^1 = \frac{\frac{3}{2}}{\frac{4}{3}} = \frac{3}{2} \times \frac{3}{4} = \frac{9}{8}$$

$$g^1a^1 \text{ is } c^1a^1 - c^1g^1 = \frac{\frac{5}{3}}{\frac{3}{2}} = \frac{5}{3} \times \frac{2}{3} = \frac{10}{9}$$

$$a^1b^1 \text{ is } c^1b^1 - c^1a^1 = \frac{\frac{15}{8}}{\frac{5}{3}} = \frac{15}{8} \times \frac{3}{5} = \frac{9}{8}$$

$$b^1c^2 \text{ is } c^1c^2 - c^1b^1 = \frac{\frac{2}{1}}{\frac{15}{8}} = \frac{2}{1} \times \frac{8}{15} = \frac{16}{15}$$

c^1	d^1	e^1	f^1	g^1	a^1	b^1	c^2
$\frac{9}{8}$	$\frac{10}{9}$	$\frac{16}{15}$	$\frac{9}{8}$	$\frac{10}{9}$	$\frac{9}{8}$	$\frac{16}{15}$	

From the above table of ratios one observes that there are three ratios for the interval of the second. The physicist names these intervals of a second as follows:

Major whole-tone is $\frac{9}{8}$
Minor whole-tone is $\frac{10}{9}$
Half-tone is $\frac{16}{15}$

The smallest interval recognized in music is the *didymic comma*, which is found by subtracting a major whole-tone from a minor whole-tone.

Comma is $\dfrac{\frac{9}{8}}{\frac{10}{9}} = \frac{9}{8} \times \frac{9}{10} = \frac{81}{80}$. The *diesis* is the difference between the major third and the minor third, which is $\dfrac{\frac{5}{4}}{\frac{6}{5}} = \frac{5}{4} \times \frac{5}{6} = \frac{25}{24}$.

The physicist derives his natural minor scale from tonic, subdominant, and dominant minor triads.

Tonic	$a : c^1 : e^1$	
Dominant	$e^1 : g^1 : b^1$	$10 : 12 : 15$
Subdominant	$d^1 : f^1 : a^1$	

Considering a as the fundamental of the key, vibration ratios can be obtained as follows:

$a^1 = 2a$

$c^1 = \frac{6}{5} a$

$e^1 = \frac{3}{2} a$

$g^1 = \frac{6}{5} e^1$; but $e^1 = \frac{3}{2} a$; then in terms of a, $g^1 = \frac{6}{5} \times \frac{3}{2} a = \frac{9}{5} a$

$b^1 = $ fifth plus fifth above $a = \frac{3}{2} \times \frac{3}{2} a = \frac{9}{4} a$; $b^1 = 2b$; therefore, $2b = \frac{9}{4} a$; $b = \frac{9}{8} a$

$d^1 = $ a perfect fifth below a^1. Knowing a and a^1, we may obtain d^1 by subtracting a fifth from the octave above a.

$$d^1 = \frac{2a}{\frac{3}{2}} = \frac{4}{3} a.$$

$f^1 = \frac{6}{5} d^1$, but d^1 is $\frac{4}{3} a$. Then $f^1 = \frac{6}{5} \times \frac{4}{3} a^1 = \frac{8}{5} a$.

Frequency	220	247.5	264	293.3	330	352	396	440
	a	b	c^1	d^1	e^1	f^1	g^1	a^1
Ratio	1	$\frac{9}{8}$	$\frac{6}{5}$	$\frac{4}{3}$	$\frac{3}{2}$	$\frac{8}{5}$	$\frac{9}{5}$	2

The interval ratio for obtaining any tone above or below any scale tone is as follows:

$$bc^1 \text{ is } ac^1 - ab \quad = \frac{\frac{6}{5}}{\frac{9}{8}} = \frac{6}{5} \times \frac{8}{9} = \frac{16}{15}$$

$$c^1 d^1 \text{ is } ad^1 - ac^1 \quad = \frac{\frac{4}{3}}{\frac{6}{5}} = \frac{4}{3} \times \frac{5}{6} = \frac{10}{9}$$

$$d^1 e^1 \text{ is } ae^1 - ad^1 \quad = \frac{\frac{3}{2}}{\frac{4}{3}} = \frac{3}{2} \times \frac{3}{4} = \frac{9}{8}$$

$$e^1 f^1 \text{ is } af^1 - ae^1 \quad = \frac{\frac{8}{5}}{\frac{3}{2}} = \frac{8}{5} \times \frac{2}{3} = \frac{16}{15}$$

$$f^1 g^1 \text{ is } ag^1 - af^1 \quad = \frac{\frac{9}{5}}{\frac{8}{5}} = \frac{9}{5} \times \frac{5}{8} = \frac{9}{8}$$

$$g^1 a^1 \text{ is } a^1 - ag^1 \quad = \frac{\frac{2}{1}}{\frac{9}{5}} = \frac{2}{1} \times \frac{5}{9} = \frac{10}{9}$$

a	b	c^1	d^1	e^1	f^1	g^1	a^1
	$\frac{9}{8}$	$\frac{16}{15}$	$\frac{10}{9}$	$\frac{9}{8}$	$\frac{16}{15}$	$\frac{9}{8}$	$\frac{10}{9}$

Based on c^1 and combining the major and minor scales, the following frequencies may be obtained:

c¹	d¹	e♭¹	e¹	f¹	g¹	a♭¹	a¹	b♭¹	b¹	c²
	$\frac{9}{8}$	$\frac{6}{5}$	$\frac{5}{4}$	$\frac{4}{3}$	$\frac{3}{2}$	$\frac{8}{5}$	$\frac{5}{3}$	$\frac{9}{5}$	$\frac{15}{8}$	$\frac{2}{1}$
264		316.8		352		422.4		475.2		528
	297		330		396		440		495	

The above just intonation accounts for ten notes within the octave. Musicians, however, use twelve notes within the octave. These notes are between c^1 and d^1, and f^1 and g^1. To obtain these notes the physicist uses the diesis. For example, to obtain $c^{1\#}$, multiply the frequency of c^1 by $\frac{25}{24}$. $c^{1\#} = \frac{25}{24} c^1$. In like manner, to obtain $d^{1\flat}$ in terms of c^1, divide d^1 by the diesis, because the pitch of d^1 is lowered.

$$d^{1\flat} = \frac{d^1}{\text{diesis}} = \frac{\frac{9}{8}c^1}{\frac{25}{24}} = \frac{9}{8} c^1 \times \frac{24}{25} = \frac{27}{25} c^1.$$

Continuing calculations of this character, one would obtain a scale of eighteen notes within the octave, based on c^1, as follows:

c¹	c¹#	d¹♭	d¹	d¹#	e¹♭	e	f¹	f¹#
1	$\frac{25}{24}$	$\frac{27}{25}$	$\frac{9}{8}$	$\frac{75}{64}$	$\frac{6}{5}$	$\frac{5}{4}$	$\frac{4}{3}$	$\frac{25}{18}$
g¹♭	g¹	g¹#	a¹♭	a¹	a¹#	b¹♭	b¹	c²
$\frac{32}{25}$	$\frac{3}{2}$	$\frac{25}{16}$	$\frac{8}{5}$	$\frac{5}{3}$	$\frac{125}{72}$	$\frac{9}{5}$	$\frac{15}{8}$	2

If scales containing 18 notes are constructed on other notes, it is easy to understand that many notes of varying frequencies will occur within a given octave. For this reason, the musical acousticians and musicians finally adopted *equal temperament*. For example, $c^{1\#}$ and $d^{1\flat}$ were to be given the same frequency. The scale of *equal temperament* has 13 notes and contains 12 equal intervals. Since musical intervals are added by multiplying them together, evidently this interval must be of such value that its 12th power is equal to 2. To obtain the frequency of any note above a given note, multiply the frequency of that note by $\sqrt[12]{2}$ or 1.05946. To obtain the frequency of the note below a given note, divide the frequency of the given note by 1.05946.

Appendix 6

NON-HARMONIC TONES RELATED TO A MINOR TRIAD

Interval	*Step*			*Step*	*Interval*

$$
\begin{array}{cc}
& A\,\natural \\[2pt]
G\!\!\nwarrow\!\!\searrow & A\,\flat \\[2pt]
F\#\!\!\nearrow &
\end{array}
$$

The tone a half-step above the third of a minor triad is spelled by the composers as a major third above the root of the triad. Theorists, likewise, agree with this spelling.

Index

A

Acoustics, 3, 307
  of chords, 307, 308
  of chromatic scale, 311
  of scales, 308
Air, column of, law, 9
Altered chord, 238
Alto range, 71
Amplitude, 13
Angle of incidence, 6
Angle of reflection, 6
Anticipation, 115
Anticlimax note, 193
Antinode, 8
Apel, Willi, 298
Appoggiatura, 115
  accented, 116
  figure, 199
Augmented second, 106
Augmented triad, 236
Authentic cadence, 143

B

Background of a beat, 20
Bar, 23
Bar-line, 23
Bass
  counterpoint, 189
  figured, 289
  fundamental, 98
  range of, 71
Beat, 19
  background, 20
  compound, 20
  conductor's, 24
  divided, 43
  simple, 20

Binary form, 299

C

Cadence, 143
  authentic, 143
  deceptive, 227
  half, 148
  imperfect authentic, 145
  imperfect plagal, 167
  perfect authentic, 143
  perfect plagal, 167
  phrygian, 269
  plagal, 167
Cantus firmus, 104
Changing tone, 116
Change of mode, 280
Chord, 69
  altered, 238
  diatonic, 102
  inversion, 69, 72, 73, 200
  progression, 129
Chromatic scale, 304
Circle of fifths, 256, 257
Clefs, 12
  classification of, 12
Climax note, 193
Closed pipe, 8, 9
Closely related key, 257
Close structure, 72
Composite wave, 14
Compound beat, 20
Compound notation, 21
Compression, 5
Conductor's beat, 24
Consonance, 59
  perfect, 60
  imperfect, 60
Consonant interval, 59
Counterpoint, 189

315